IMAGES
of America

NCA&T vs. NCCU
More Than Just a Game

Eagles and Aggies square off in Durham at O'Kelly-Riddick Stadium in 2016. (Courtesy of North Carolina Central University Athletics Department.)

ON THE COVER: Pictured is the old swing pass. North Carolina Agricultural & Technical College defeated an undefeated North Carolina College team in Durham to win the Central Intercollegiate Athletic Association in 1958. (Courtesy of the North Carolina Collection Photographic Archives, The Wilson Library, University of North Carolina at Chapel Hill.)

ON THE BACK COVER, LEFT: Dr. James E. Shepard, founder and president of North Carolina Central from 1910 to 1947. (Courtesy of Andre Vann, coordinator of University Archives, North Carolina Central University Archives – James E. Shepard Memorial Library.)

ON THE BACK COVER, RIGHT: Dr. James B. Dudley, president of North Carolina A&T from 1896 to 1925. (Courtesy of James Stewart, university archivist, North Carolina A&T State University Archives and Special Collections.)

IMAGES
of America

NCA&T vs. NCCU
More Than Just a Game

Charles D. Johnson and Arwin D. Smallwood

ARCADIA
PUBLISHING

Published by Arcadia Publishing
Charleston, South Carolina

Printed in the United States of America

Library of Congress Control Number: 2023941589

For all general information, please contact Arcadia Publishing:
Telephone 843-853-2070
Fax 843-853-0044
E-mail sales@arcadiapublishing.com

Visit us on the Internet at www.arcadiapublishing.com

ACKNOWLEDGMENTS

Completing this book would not have been possible without the support of many special people and institutions. Special thanks to James Stewart, University Archivist at North Carolina Agricultural and Technical State University (NCA&T), and Andre Vann, Coordinator of University Archives at North Carolina Central University (NCCU), for providing access to archival collections, campus newspapers, annuals, photographs, and media guides. We thank Patrick C. Cullom, Visual and Material Processing Archivist, and Rebecca Stubbs-Carter, Visual Materials Processing Assistant, in Wilson Library at the University of North Carolina at Chapel Hill, for guiding us through the Durham Herald Co. Newspaper Photograph Collection. We would also like to thank Evonda Haith (NCA&T) and Beverly Barnes Evans, who gave valued assistance with oral interviews. Rodney Dawson gave his time and talent to create a short documentary of A&T football to contribute to our efforts, and we are grateful to him. We are thankful for the help of Darren Wellman and Kimberly Cheek at NCA&T, who mentored and supervised undergraduate research assistants. We are grateful to them as well. In particular, Ashanti Gaydon (NCA&T) and Naitara Matthews (NCCU) gave their time and talents. We are particularly grateful to Kamilah Henry Williams, an undergraduate researcher at NCA&T at the start of this book project and now a graduate student in the Public History Program at NCCU. We also thank Khadija McNair (NCCU) for her contribution to mining archives and collecting materials for this book. Photos are at the heart of this book, and we wish to thank Dr. Michael Simmons (NCA&T) for allowing us to use some of his outstanding photographs. We would be remiss if we did not give special thanks to Doug Burt of Doug Burt Photography and Kevin L. Dorsey of Kevin L. Dorsey Photography for their excellent work in preserving both schools' football and athletic histories through their photographs. Many hands make light work and Atty. Eric Montgomery (NCCU) has been with us from the start. He has contributed parts of his enormous collection of historical documents related to the rivalry, his financial resources, and his time. For all of that, we say thank you. Finally, we are most grateful to the many former coaches, players, and alumni who contributed to this work.

CONTENTS

PREFACE

For an African American child in the early 1970s, whether growing up within walking distance of North Carolina Central University (NCCU) or North Carolina Agricultural and Technical State University (NCA&T), in rural eastern, central, or western North Carolina, in one of the many small towns like Tarboro, Warsaw, or Thomasville, or in big cities like Wilmington, Raleigh, Winston-Salem, or Charlotte, this game was "The Game." Many have fond memories of NCCU and NCA&T football games. For the Johnson family and many of the African American residents of Durham, NCCU and NCA&T football games were an important social event. They brought us together and reinforced the idea that we were part of a vibrant and active community. As youngsters, we could not have known, as we do now, that along with North Carolina Mutual Life Insurance Company, Mechanics and Farmers Bank, and Lincoln Hospital, NCCU was a cornerstone of a thriving and, in many ways, unique Black community. For the Smallwood family, far removed from either Durham or Greensboro in rural northeastern North Carolina, the impact of both schools was just as profound. With farming being the main industry in the region, there was hardly a family that did not benefit in some way from the NCA&T agricultural extension agents and home economics teachers teaching both food preservation and cultivation. Also, there was hardly a household that did not have an insurance policy from North Carolina Mutual Insurance Company, the largest Black-owned insurance company in the world for most of the 20th century, and it must be noted that it was founded by many of the same individuals who founded NCCU. In both Durham and Greensboro, as well as around the state, African American residents had seemingly innumerable ties to both schools as alumni or employees or partners, and they were inseparable from the community—the institutions were and are both the community, and the community is each institution—this included the surrounding communities as well. Dr. John Mayfield, who was born in Thomasville, noted that "you knew when the game was in Greensboro because the streets of Thomasville were deserted because everyone had gone to the game." When the Eagles of NCCU had a home football game, it was the same—the African American community in and near Durham showed up. We both learned that when NCCU played the Aggies of NCA&T, it seemed like the entire state of North Carolina showed up. Indeed, because of racial segregation, which did not end legally until the mid-1960s, for much of the 20th century, the Eagles vs. Aggies football game was the biggest single-day entertainment event for African Americans in the state of North Carolina. This is because NCCU and NCA&T are the two largest HBCUs in the state, and both institutions have alumni in communities across the state and the nation. But it was not just the size of the fanbases that made the rivalry so significant, it was also the intensity of the games.

Preparation for the game began at the final whistle of the previous game, sometimes earlier. Long before game day, Eagles and Aggies laid plans and talked of the game. A mention of a new player, a potential difference maker, or a coach on the hot seat was often at the center of conversations, but strategies for parking, attire, and pregame rituals also had to be attended to. On game day, a carnival-like atmosphere enveloped the game site as fans from both schools were everywhere. Eagles clad with maroon and gray and Aggies decked out in blue and gold made their way along streets leading toward the stadium; some stopped to patronize vendors peddling an assortment of tasty foods or colorful paraphernalia, while others joined a tailgate to enjoy laughs and good eating with friends old and new. From charcoal grills and food tables, the inviting aroma of barbecue ribs, barbecue chicken, brisket, hotdogs, hamburgers, fried fish, potato salad, and coleslaw coalesced and flowed throughout the tailgate section. Grill masters, some fathers bedecked in white- or team-colored aprons, cooked and served up the food while talking and laughing with family and friends, many of whom remained in the tailgate section throughout the game. Signaling game time was approaching, off in the distance at first, the percussive sound of the marching band tantalizes and rises. Out in front, the drum majors and majorettes keep in step with the band and captivate the crowd with rhythmic dance moves, high knees, and big arm movements. As they lead to the stadium, fans of both teams line the streets along the band's course. Children squeeze in front of their parents to get a better view, while people weave through the adjacent crowd making their way to the stadium.

More than just a game, the annual fall meeting on the gridiron between NCCU in Durham and NCA&T in Greensboro is one of the biggest rivalries in HBCU sports, in both fan following and in revenue generated. Only 50 miles apart from each other, NCA&T and NCCU recruit many of the same students and student-athletes. In fact, many families have alumni from both schools. This close familiarity fuels the rivalry and its emotional appeal. At the heart of the rivalry is the more extensive statement the game makes about which school is better and, by extension, which body of students, faculty, and administrators is better. Indeed, the rivalry extends well beyond the sidelines of the football field itself, deep into the households, and the hearts, of alumni and fans of both schools.

NCA&T and NCCU are historically Black universities with long and rich histories. Their origins are tied to the African American quest for equal educational opportunity despite Black students being excluded from nearly all white colleges in the United States during the 19th and early 20th centuries. After the end of the Civil War and the adoption of the 13th Amendment ending slavery, African Americans sought land and education. Land was denied to most African Americans, but the creation of historically Black colleges and universities opened formal higher education to African Americans. Cheyney State University, founded in 1837 in Cheyney, Pennsylvania, was the first HBCU. North Carolina A&T, a land-grant institution, was founded in 1891, and North Carolina Central University opened in 1910. Both schools have undergone multiple name changes, reflecting their growth and maturation. Because of racial segregation, Black college football teams played in separate leagues from predominantly white teams and played for a separate national title.

A 1985 photograph shows drum majors Randolph Henderson of NCCU (left) and Roosevelt Pratt of NCA&T (right). Henderson and Pratt are best friends and were in the band at Fayetteville E.E. Smith High School. (Courtesy of Roosevelt Pratt.)

INTRODUCTION

IRON SHARPENS IRON

NCA&T and NCCU are the two most prominent HBCUs in North Carolina and among the most prominent in the nation. Their football rivalry is not the oldest. Biddle University, today Johnson C. Smith University, and Livingstone College, two North Carolina schools, played in the first football game between HBCUs in 1892, a 4-0 Biddle victory. But the Aggie-Eagle rivalry is the largest in the state.

NCA&T was established in 1891. It came about to satisfy the requirements of the 1890 Morrill Act, which "prohibited the distribution of money to states that made distinctions of race in admissions unless at least one land-grant college for African Americans was established." In response, the State of North Carolina placed a temporary agricultural program at Shaw University, a private Baptist HBCU in Raleigh. The agricultural program was a stepping-stone to creating an agricultural and mechanical school for the Colored race in North Carolina. Its formation had been made necessary by the creation in 1887 of North Carolina's first land-grant institution, the whites-only North Carolina College of Agriculture and Mechanic Arts, located in Raleigh. Now North Carolina State University (NCSU), it was a progeny of the 1862 Morrill Act, which provided 30,000 acres of federal land to states for each member of Congress from the state as of the 1860 federal census. NCSU was chartered in 1887 and began operation in 1889. The 1890 Morrill Act forced state legislators to establish an agricultural and mechanical training school for the Colored race. Durham, Greensboro, Raleigh, Winston-Salem, and Wilmington bid for the agricultural and mechanical school. Greensboro won the bid to establish the school with the support of African American business leaders and the Warnersville community. For most of the 20th century, its mission was agricultural and mechanical training.

NCCU was founded in 1910. Dr. James E. Shepard established the National Religious Training School and Chautauqua in 1910 to educate African American ministers. Dr. Shepard was born in Raleigh in 1875, graduated from Shaw University, and in 1900 began serving as field secretary for the International Sunday School Association (ISSA). When Shepard joined the ISSA at the turn of the century, it provided religious instruction for 11 million children and adults in the United States. His ISSA experiences informed his decision to establish a school for religious training. Reflecting nascent growth, in 1911, "Chautauqua" was dropped from the name, and four years later, "Religious" was dropped, but the institution's core mission remained the same.

Thus, the name became the National Training School (NTS). NTS traveled to Greensboro to take on the Aggies for the first time in the fall of 1922. The school continued to evolve, and in 1923, the name was changed to the Durham State Normal School to reflect its new teacher training mission. In 1925, the State of North Carolina purchased the school, renaming it the North Carolina College for Negroes at Durham. In 1947, "for Negroes" was dropped. The final name change came in 1969, when the institution became North Carolina Central University, again reflecting growth and expansion.

In this c. 1900 photograph, students keep the grounds before the impressive James Benson Dudley Hall. Constructed in 1893, a fire destroyed it in 1930. The present Dudley Building opened in 1931. (Courtesy of North Carolina A&T State University Archives and Special Collections.)

Dr. James Benson Dudley was a career educator. Before going to A&T in 1896, for 15 years, he was a principal at the Peabody Graded School in Wilmington. A charismatic statesman, Dudley skillfully navigated A&T through its early development to the point where the institution was on a firm financial footing at the time of his passing in 1925. (Courtesy of North Carolina A&T State University Archives and Special Collections.)

Dr. James Edward Shepard was the son of Rev. Augustus Shepard and Hattie Whitted Shepard. In 1900, he began serving as field secretary for the ISSA. His International Sunday School Association (ISSA) experiences informed his decision to establish the National Religious Training School and Chautauqua, a school for religious training for African Americans. (Courtesy of North Carolina Central University Archives–James E. Shepard Memorial Library.) Originally called the Clyde R. Hoey Administration Building after the North Carolina governor who served from 1937 to 1941, the North Carolina Central University Board of Trustees voted to rename the building in honor of Dr. James E. Shepard in 2019. Student protests led by Ajamu Dillahunt significantly influenced the name change. (Courtesy of North Carolina Central University Archives–James E. Shepard Memorial Library.)

One

ROOTS OF THE RIVALRY
1922–1939

In 1922, the A&T Aggies and the NCC Eagles played on Dudley Field in Greensboro for the first time. A&T won the initial meeting between the two largest HBCUs in the state by a score of 26-0. A large and enthusiastic crowd watched the game, and over the course of the 20th century, thousands of fans, including many of the most prominent Blacks in the state, attended the games.

Between 1922 and 1939, the Eagles and Aggies played 15 times. The Aggies won nine of those games, and the teams tied once. Lonnie P. Byarm, who coached A&T until 1929, was 4-0-1 against the Eagles, guided the Aggies into the then–Colored Intercollegiate Athletic Association (CIAA) in 1924, and won the conference title in 1927. In the 1920s, Herman "Bus" Coleman starred for A&T and was selected All-CIAA three times (1925–1927) as a halfback. Inman Breaux coached the Aggies from 1930 to 1935 and 1937 to 1938. He compiled a record of 4-2 against NCC. A&T quarterback McHenry Norman was a standout player for Breaux in the 1930s and, in 1934, scored on a 100-yard punt return that ended NCC's four-game win streak against A&T (1930–1933). Norman was selected All-CIAA in 1934.

Wilson Vashon Eagleson, a 1920 Indiana University graduate, was NCC's first coach in the series. In 1924, Eagleson tied the Aggies 13-13 and posted a 4-2-1 record. His final year coaching for NCC was in 1926. Frances Marshall Eagleson, his wife, was a longtime and beloved registrar at NCC. Their son Wilson Vashon Eagleson Jr. was one of the first Tuskegee Airmen. Coach Leo Townsend, a former coach of Hillside High School in Durham, was the first NCC coach to boast a winning record against A&T. Townsend was 4-2 in the series, and his teams won four in a row between 1930 and 1933. Future NCC coach Herman Riddick played end for Townsend and was team captain in 1931. The teams played on Thanksgiving for the first time in 1932 in Greensboro, and the annual game became known as the Thanksgiving Day Classic. Early stars for the Eagles include end Irwin "Bus" Holmes, quarterback Bill Malone, and halfback Wauna Dooms. Holmes and Dooms were Pennsylvanians.

HBCU bands are a significant part of the overall HBCU game experience. Bands from both schools began providing halftime entertainment during this period. In 1937, the *Norfolk Journal and Guide* reported that NCC had a high-stepping female drum major at the head of its band, and A&T fielded "a smartly uniformed, colorful band."

Born in 1889 in Goose Creek, Union County, North Carolina, Lonnie Pfunander Byarm grew up on a farm, became a scientist, served in World War I, and was an Aggie sports pioneer. Byarm graduated in 1911 from the Agricultural and Mechanical College for the Colored Race, as A&T was then known, with a bachelor of science degree. Following graduation, Byarm joined the faculty of A&M College. He taught machine drawing, machine drawing and design, gas engines, and engine handling. As head football coach of the Aggies, he never lost to the Eagles, and in 1927, he coached A&T to its first CIAA title. (Courtesy of North Carolina A&T State University Archives and Special Collections.)

In 1922, Wilson Vashon Eagleson Sr. became the first Eagles coach to compete against the farmers in training. The agriculturalists or Aggies whipped the National Training School 26-0. Eagleson was born in Indiana in 1898, but his great-grandparents migrated to Indiana from Chatham County, North Carolina. They had Tuscarora blood, were free people of color, and moved to the Lost Creek Settlement in Vigo County, Indiana. His father, Preston, was the first African American football player at the University of Indiana. His wife, Frances Marshall Eagleson, was the first African American female graduate from the University of Indiana and served as registrar at NCCU for three decades (1928–1964). His son Wilson Vashon Eagleson Jr. was a Tuskegee Airman. Eagleson's best year as head coach of NCC was 1924. The Eagles went 4-2-1 and tied A&T. He stepped down as head coach in 1926 to pursue graduate education. In 1930, Eagleson joined the staff of Harry Jefferson at A&T. He died in a car accident in 1933. (Courtesy of Ancestry.com.)

In 1922, the National Training School, as NCCU was then known, and A&T played at James B. Dudley Field in Greensboro, and the Aggies won 26-0. The Black press closely covered HBCU football. This is a summary from the *Norfolk Journal and Guide* for December 9, 1922. In addition to giving game highlights, it also gives the starting lineups. (Courtesy of the *New Journal and Guide*.)

A. & T. Wins From National Training

Greensboro, N. C.—A. and T. College showed her superiority in football over the National Training School from Durham by making three touchdowns and two successful trys for points after touchdown in the first half. The second half was played with mostly second string men who were eager to get into the fray. Both teams played hard, but clean ball. The first half ended with the ball in A. and T.'s possession on the forty yard line and the score standing 20 to 0 for A. and T.

Skirts of both flanks and the line plunging of Captain Howell did much ground gaining for the locals whose goal was never in danger from time of the whistle to start the game until the whistle that notified the battling teams that the playing time was over. In the third quarter another touchdown was added to A. and T.'s side, as a result of consistent ground gaining through the visitor's line. Trick plays and passes were the oustanding features of the visitor's style of attack; but they were solved by the hawk eyes of A. and T.'s back men. Howell, Bell, Brown and Lane did stellar work for the winners; while Nutal, Wilson and Cofield, did the best work for the losers.

LINEUP AND SUMMARY

A. and T., 26	Position	N. T. S., 0
Lane	L. E.	Sparrow
Hyman	L. T.	O'Kelly
Blaine	L. G.	Jackson, A.
Patterson	C.	Buzby
Cunningham	R. G.	Bullock
Spaulding	R. T.	Harris
Brown	R. E.	Wilson
Bell, M.	Q. B.	Nutall
Bell, E.	R. H.	Coefield
Chavis	L. H.	Alston
Howell	F. B.	Smith

Referee, Dr. Hargraves, Shaw; umpire, Jones, Biddle; headlinesman, Riddick, A. and T. Time fifteen minute periods.

A&T did not play NCC but won games against in-state HBCUs and earned its first North Carolina Athletic Conference state title in 1923. This *Norfolk Journal and Guide* newspaper clipping announces A&T as champions of the North Carolina Athletic Conference. A&T's rivals in Durham undoubtedly noted that the Aggies did not play them and that they won the championship. (Courtesy of the *New Journal and Guide*.)

SATURDAY, DECEMBER 22, 1923

NORFOLK JOURNAL AND GUIDE

A. & T. COLLEGE WINS N. C. STATE TITLE

Undefeated In State; Bell Named as Captain for Season of 1924.

Greensboro, N. C.—"They shall not pass." With this as it slogan, backed by grim and dogged determination, A. and T's. terrible machine swept through North Carolina at whirlwind speed—and they did not pass. So, when the curtain fell Thanksgiving day, 1923, on one of the most sensational seasons in the history of the institution, which ended in a 10-0 defeat over Bennett, A. and T. found herself in a position to which she had aspired through long years of patience plodding, but which had hiterto not attained—the championship in football in the North Carolina Athletic Conference.

The season was opened on October 6th by an invasion of Howard's territory. Doubt, misgiving and prophecy of overwhelming defeat were in the air when the Aggies faced their heavier opponents. But though we failed to score, the power of our attack was well reflected in the fact that Howard was held to a single touchdown, and this, when compared with our 30-0 defeat in 1921 and a 40-0 defeat in 1922, was indeed encouraging.

Our campaign in the State opened on October 12, with a 10-0 victory over Shaw, and as a result hope was quickened, for Shaw was reckoned as our most formidable opponent.

Biddle was the next to meet

us, and after a stiff fight, suffered a 20-0 defeat.

Buoyed up by victory, the Aggies repulsed the attack of the game eleven representing St. Augustine and turned them back with a 30-0 defeat.

A sudden break came in the team's winning streak, when on November third, it was defeated by a score of 7-0 by V. N. I. I. at Petersburg. The Hilltoppers were held scoreless up to the last minutes of play. Threatening advances were made upon the Virginian's line, but forward passes which failed of execution, lost for us our chances to score.

Undaunted, the machine returned and rode over Palmer Institute to a 116-0 victory. This was perhaps the most unique game of the season. The visitors were unquestionably outclassed, but they were game and put up a hard fight to the end. Every man on the Aggie lineup was sent into the fray and scoring was so rapid and sensational that writer would be fairly safe in saying that every man on the team scored a touchdown.

Claflin University of Orangeburg, South Carolina, had dreams of being the invincible champions of the South. But

"Of all the sad words of tongue or pen,

The saddest are these—IT MIGHT HAVE BEEN."

Having defeated some of the best teams in the south, Claflin's was apparently clear to an easy victory over A. and T. But after a hard and gruelling contest, her dream was shattered, and she had to be content with a 21-0 defeat.

When Bennett met A. and T., on Thanksgiving Day, though the former had carried a light schedule, and made all but a shining record, and the latter had proved supreme in the State, the outcome was more doubtful than at any time since the event became a classic. And never did the two team's play harder, nor under more unfavorable conditions, for a steady rain was falling and the field was

slippery to a point as to make footing insecure.

In the first half, the teams deadlocked to a scoreless tie. In the third quarter, A. and T. crossed Bennett's line for the only touchdown made in the game. In the final period, Coleman's faithful toe secured for A. and T. a field goal from the 30 yard line, bringing the score to 10-0 in A. and T.'s favor. It was a hard fought battle, and happy to relate, A. andT. wrote "Q. E. D." after one of the finest pieces of work she has accomplished for some time.

Thus ended A. and T.'s most brilliant season on the gridiron. Her success, though involving many things, can be directly traced to one element in particular—TEAMWORK. Never did a machine work with greater precision. Though our aerial attack was weak at times, the line attack was unquestionably strong and effective, while our own line was held impregnable.

In every machine there are always certain elements that attract the eye and are more outstanding than others. The same is true of a football team. Though a team may work as a well-oiled machine and the players composing that team may work as one, there are always members that stand out from their fellows. And the eleven representing A. and T. was no exception. Never did an army have a more efficient general, nor did a general receive more hearty co-operation from his colleagues than our own Malachi Bell, who at quarter, was a joy to us and one to be feared by our opponents.

Some wise person has said that the only person that kicks all the time and gets along with folks is a chorus girl. But Harry ("Bust") Coleman, playing left half, kicked, and kicked hard, and in so doing, won fame for his team and a place in the hearts of every local football fan. He came to us for the first time this year, and proved that the Old Dominion can raise football stars as well as goobers.

A. & T. HELD TO A 13-13 DEADLOCK BY DUR'M STATE

Durham, N. C., Nov. 22—With A. & T. College of Greensboro coming to Durham very much overrated, the fast Durham State Normal eleven engaged in a battle royal which ended in a 13-13 tie.

With A. & T. displaying a wonderful four man shift over "Brick" O'Kelly's tackle and gaining little ground their efforts would have been futile had it not been for luck in aiding to draw first blood in the third period. Coleman kicking off to State Normal, assisted by a high wind sent the oval far beyond the State Normal goal line A. & T. fleet-footed ends recovered for their first touchdown. Before State could survive from the effects of this sting, Bell for A. & T. raced around right end for 30 yards to score the second touchdown of the encounter. Coleman drop-kicked for the extra point. Score A. & T. 13, State Normal 0.

With blood in their eyes, the flying squadron resorted to the air and in the twinkling of an eye Harris speared a pass from Alston and raced 30 yards across for State's first touchdown. Stroud failed to drop-kicked for the extra point. With "Cute" Coward cal-

burg Seminary 12-9 and St. Augustine 32-0.

THE LINEUP

A. & T.—13		Durham S. N.—13
Hester	L. E.	Wilson, W.
Lane	L. T.	O'Kelley
Coles	L. G.	Brooks
Patterson	C.	Hammond
Brown	R. G.	Jones
Cunningh'm	R. T.	Caldwell
Miller	R. E.	Wilson, M.
Bell	Q. B.	Coward
Wilson	L. H.	Alston
Coleman	R. H.	Harris
Lane, J.	F. B.	Stroud

Referee: Lewis, (Morehouse); umpire, Blackman, (Howard); headlinesman, Oxley, (Harvard).

ling signals at a rapid clip State Normal carried on in grand style, when two incompleted passes had been grounded, W. Wilson accepted a perfect throw from Stroud and raced 45 yards before being downed by Lane. With the ball resting comfortably on A. & T.'s 5 yard line Stroud the "human battering ram" dug a hole in A. & T.'s line for six points, he also performed the same feat for the extra point.

By reason of tieing A. & T. and winning every game played in the State gives Durham State Normal a decided edge on St. Paul for the Turkey Day Classic. State Normal has lost only one game during the present season, that being the one to Hampton in their first clash of the season by a score of 32-0, winning from Bennett College 6-0, Livingstone College 13-0, Lynch-

In 1924, in a surprise outcome, upstart Durham State Normal School managed a 13-13 tie against the Aggies in Durham—a *Norfolk Journal and Guide* summary of the game includes the starting lineups. (Courtesy of the *New Journal and Guide*.)

In 1924, the Durham State football team posted its best record. The Eagles finished the season 4-2-1. Head coach Wilson Vashon Eagleson is standing at left. (Courtesy of North Carolina Central University Archives–James E. Shepard Memorial Library.)

Coach Eagleson   FOOTBALL TEAM 1924

In 1925, A&T played its first season in the CIAA, and coach Lonnie Byarm and the Aggies walloped the visiting Eagles 19-0 in Greensboro. Freshman halfback Herman "Bus" Coleman starred for A&T. A game summary from the *Norfolk Journal and Guide* for includes the starting lineups. At the end of the season, Coleman became the first Aggie named to the All-CIAA team. (Courtesy of the *New Journal and Guide*.)

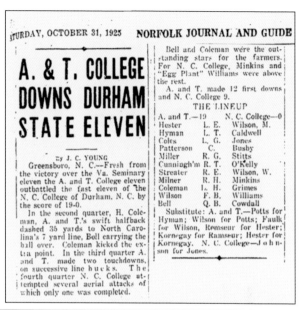

SATURDAY, OCTOBER 31, 1925 — NORFOLK JOURNAL AND GUIDE

A. & T. COLLEGE DOWNS DURHAM STATE ELEVEN

By J. C. YOUNG

Greensboro, N. C.—Fresh from the victory over the Va. Seminary eleven the A. and T. College eleven outbattled the fast eleven of the N. C. College of Durham, N. C. by the score of 19-0.

In the second quarter, H. Coleman, A. and T.'s swift halfback dashed 35 yards to North Carolina's 7 yard line, Bell carrying the ball over. Coleman kicked the extra point. In the third quarter A. and T. made two touchdowns, on successive line bucks. The fourth quarter N. C. College attempted several aerial attacks of which only one was completed.

Bell and Coleman were the outstanding stars for the farmers. For N. C. College, Minkins and "Egg Plant" Williams were above the rest.

A. and T. made 12 first downs and N. C. College 9.

THE LINEUP

A. and T.—19		N. C. College—0
Hester	L. E.	Wilson, M.
Hyman	L. T.	Caldwell
Coles	L. G.	Jones
Patterson	C.	Busby
Miller	R. G.	Stitts
Cunningh'm	R. T.	O'Kelly
Streater	R. E.	Wilson, W.
Milner	R. H.	Minkins
Coleman	L. H.	Grimes
Wilson	F. B.	Williams
Bell	Q. B.	Cowdall

Substitute: A. and T.—Potts for Hyman; Wilson for Potts; Faulk for Wilson, Remseur for Hester; Kornegay for Ramseur; Hester for Kornegay. N. C. College—Johnson for Jones.

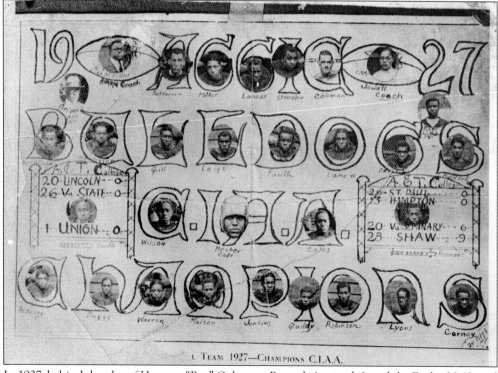

In 1927, behind the play of Herman "Bus" Coleman, Byarm's Aggies defeated the Eagles 28-13, and in Durham, Dave M. Waters was named head coach at North Carolina College for Negroes. The Eagles faced the strongest A&T football team in the school's history. A 1927 team poster celebrates A&T's first-ever CIAA championship. The Aggies shut out five of their eight opponents. Their lone loss was to eventual HBCU national champion Bluefield State. Four Aggies were named All-CIAA: Herman Coleman, halfback; Jessie Miller, guard; M.E. Patterson, center; and J.A. Streeter, end. (Courtesy of North Carolina A&T State University Archives and Special Collections.)

AGGIES CLIP WINGS OF N. C. EAGLES, 20-0

Lane, As Triple Threat, Hogs Limelight With Two Touch-downs

WINSTON-SALEM. —Without the services of "Bus" Coleman, All-American triple threat ace, A. and T.'s Aggie Bulldogs over-whelmingly defeated the North Carolina State College eleven, here, Saturday afternoon by a score of 20 to 0.

In 1928, the game was played in Winston-Salem, and James Freeman "Horse" Lane scored two touchdowns in leading the Aggies to a 20-0 victory over NCC. For the first time in coverage of the games played against A&T, the press began referring to NCC as the Eagles. This game headline is from the October 20, 1928, *Afro-American* newspaper. (Courtesy of the *Afro-American*.)

James Freeman "Horse" Lane was a standout halfback for A&T. He was named All-CIAA in 1928. Professionally, Lane was a school teacher. He was born in Raleigh in 1900 and died in 1965. (Courtesy of the James F. Lane family.)

L. A. TOWNSEND IS NAMED COACH AT N. C. COLLEGE

Replaces "Birdie" Crudup As Mentor Of Eagles

DURHAM, N. C.—L. A. Townsend who for the past several years has coached the successful Hillside Football team, has been named as Coach at North Carolina College.

Coach Townsend has just returned from attendance at a Coaching School at Witenberg College, Springfield, Ohio.

The new coach is a graduate of North Carolina College and of Howard University; having played Football, Baseball and Basketball during his College years.

Coach Townsend says that his two major objectives this fall are to beat Howard at Washington, Nov. 8, and Lincoln at Durham, Oct. 4.

The Lincoln game will bring a host of out-of-town visitors and already, extensive plans are being made to entertain them and to make this one of the outstanding events of the football season.

In 1930, Harry "Big Jeff" Jefferson became the head coach at A&T. Jefferson had won HBCU national championships at Bluefield State in 1927 and 1928. NCC hired Leo Townsend away from Hillside High School in Durham as its head coach. But Townsend bested Jefferson in 1930, and the Eagles defeated A&T for the first time by a score of 20-14. Future legendary NCC head coach Herman Riddick played end for NCC in 1930. (Courtesy of the *New Journal and Guide*.)

In 1931, NCC defeated A&T in Greensboro 6-0. Coach Townsend moved Irwin Holmes to quarterback, and the elusive Pennsylvania native and Herman Riddick bedeviled the Bulldog defense the entire afternoon. The victory earned NCC the North Carolina State Championship. Zora Neale Hurston is pictured here at an NCC football game. Hurston is widely considered one of the greatest writers of the 20th century. She was a professor in the Drama Department at NCC in the late 1930s. (Courtesy of North Carolina Central University Archives–James E. Shepard Memorial Library.)

The teams played on Thanksgiving Day for the first time in 1932. A&T replaced head coach Harry Jefferson with Inman Breaux, but NCC won 20-0 and extended its win streak to three straight against the Aggies. NCC's Irwin Holmes scored two touchdowns, and Bill Malone scored one for the Eagles. Game officials lost track of downs and gifted the visiting Eagles an improbable fifth down. Bill Malone took advantage of their mistake and scored a touchdown. (Courtesy of the *Afro-American*.)

SAY OFFICIALS SLEPT IN A. & T.- N.C. STATE GAME

GREENSBORO, N.C.—The Flying Eagles of N.C. State College soared high over the A. and T. College Aggies to a 19-0 victory here on Thanksgiving Day.

Dr. James E. Shepard was convinced that for NCC to compete at the highest level of Black college football, he had to recruit players from the Midwest. In 1930, he recruited Irwin Holmes Sr. (pictured) from Pittsburgh, Pennsylvania, a football hotbed, to NCC. Holmes led NCC to four consecutive victories over A&T. Holmes's son, Irwin Jr., a Hillside High School graduate, was the first African American graduate of North Carolina State University and the first African American athlete in the Atlantic Coast Conference. (Courtesy of the Irwin R. Holmes Jr. family.)

N.C. COLLEGE EAGLES ANNEX STATE TITLE, DEFEAT BULLDOGS, 20 TO 0

Dooms, Malone and Holmes Sprint 40, 60 And 40 Yards To Score

DUHRAM, N. C.—In the annual Thanksgiving day classic played in the college park, the North Carolina Eagles clinched its fourth state football championship by soundly trimming the strong A. and T. Aggies, from Greensboro, by the score of 20 to 0.

Supported by a stalwart forward wall, Malonee and Dooms, Eagle backfield men, time after time tore off yardage that spelled defeat to the visiting eleven.

Early in the second quarter, Malone side-stepped and eluded would-be Aggie tacklers and sprinted 40 yards for the initial score of the day. Several minutes later, Dooms scored on a 60 yard jaunt after the Aggies were held in midfield for downs. Malone kicked the extra point from placement after each touchdown.

Irvin Holmes, captain and end of the North Carolina Eagles, snatched a pass from Malone and ran 40 yards to register the final score in the second period. The try for extra point failed.

The work of Holmes climaxed a season of outstanding football playing and probably labels him for a position on the all-CIAA outfit.

Neither team was able to score during the second half as both eleven relied on an aerial show. Morrow, visiting back, Harbison, and Pittman, starred in the line.

Holmes, Palmer, Dickerson, and Alston played good ball in addition to the Eagle backfield.

Called the Thanksgiving Day Classic for the first time, the game played in Durham ended in a 20-0 NCC victory. Irwin Holmes, Wauna Dooms, and Bill Malone scored touchdowns for the Eagles. The win was the fourth in a row for NCC and the team's third straight shutout of A&T. The outstanding play of team captain Holmes, Dooms, and Malone are apparent in this game summary from the December 9, 1933, *Norfolk Journal and Guide*. Holmes and Malone finished their careers 4-0 versus A&T. (Courtesy of the *New Journal and Guide*.)

A Navy veteran of World War II, William Paul "Bill" Malone was born in Montgomery, Alabama, in 1910. A versatile athlete from 1930 to 1933, Malone played halfback and quarterback for NCC. He excelled at both positions and was a difference-maker against the Aggies every time they played. Malone was an employee of North Carolina Mutual Life Insurance Company for four decades. (Courtesy of the Irwin R. Holmes Jr. family.)

In 1934, Coach Inman Breaux fielded the second-best team in A&T's history behind Byarm's 1927 CIAA championship team. The Aggies' lone loss was to perennial power Morgan State. Breaux was one of the fastest players in the CIAA when he played quarterback for Virginia Union, and he recruited speed to A&T. Aggie quarterback McHenry Norman returned an Eagles punt 100 yards for the decisive touchdown and a 6-0 victory. Pictured is the *Afro-American* newspaper headline for December 9, 1934. (Courtesy of the *Afro-American*.)

A. and T. Routs N.C. State, 6-0, Thanksgiving Day

GREENSBORO, N.C.—A 100-yard run for a touchdown by Norman, quarterback for the A. and T. Aggies was the slim margin by which the Breaux-coached gridders defeated the North Carolina Eagles, here Thanksgiving Day, before 1,500 spectators.

Few quarterbacks in the 1930s bedeviled the Eagles the way A&T's McHenry Norman did. An Oklahoman with exceptional athleticism and speed, Norman carried A&T to a huge upset victory over the Eagles as a freshman and won four in a row against NCC, including a record-setting 39-0 drubbing of the Eagles in 1936. (Courtesy of McHenry "Skip" Norman III.)

McHenry Norman married the beautiful and talented Maidie Ruth Gamble, a Bennett College coed who became a Hollywood movie actress. Gamble appeared in such films as *The Well* (1951), *Torch Song* (1953), *Bright Road* (1953), *Susan Slept Here* (1954), *The Opposite Sex* (1956), *Written on the Wind* (1956), and *Whatever Happened to Baby Jane?* (1962). (Courtesy of McHenry "Skip" Norman III.)

BULLDOGS RALLY TO STOP EAGLES IN HOMECOMING

Graham and Norman In Starring Roles As State Bows, 9-0

DURHAM, N. C. — Before a Homecoming day crowd of 2,000 football fans, the N. C. College Eagles repulsed every scoring threat of the A. and T. College Bulldogs for 40 minutes then saw the defense weaken long enough to allow Woody Graham, Aggie fullback, to score the only touchdown of the game from the one foot mark. Norman's try for the extra point failed.

In 1935, A&T defeated NCC in Durham 9-0. Aggies fullback Woody Graham took a handoff from McHenry Norman and plunged in for an A&T touchdown. Norman added a field goal in the fourth quarter to end the scoring. A&T finished the season in third place with a record of 6-2-1. In 1935, the game was played on NCC's homecoming for the first time. (Courtesy of the *New Journal and Guide*.)

Case Settled In 3 Minutes; A. & T. Forfeits Grid Games For Playing Ineligible Men

A special CIAA committee determined that two A&T football players, Walter D. Calvin and Harry Evans Lash, had transferred in and played immediately, violating conference rules. A&T's coaches were unaware that Calvin and Lash had previously played for other teams. A&T vacated all its victories in which Calvin or Lash played, including the win over NCC. In the late 1930s, Lash was the high school track coach of the 1948 Olympic gold medal winner Alice Coachman, the first African American woman to win a gold medal. (Courtesy of the *New Journal and Guide*.)

Harry Lash, a former Aggie football player, was the high school track coach of Alice Marie Coachman (pictured) in Georgia. Coachman was the first African American woman to win an Olympic Gold Medal, doing so in 1948 in London. Her high jump of 5 feet 6 1/8 inches also set an Olympic record. (Courtesy of the *New York Amsterdam News*.)

The Afro-American December 5, 1936. Page 27

A. and T. 39;
N. C. State 0

Played before 5,000 spectators, A&T defeated NCC 39-0 in 1936 in Greensboro, the largest margin of victory in the rivalry at that time. Coach Inman Breaux took a leave of absence for the 1936 season, so Samuel Barksdale, an assistant coach, took his place. Edward Haygood "Buddy" Adams, the basketball coach at NCC, replaced Townsend. The game headline from the *Afro-American* newspaper shows the Thanksgiving Day massacre of North Carolina College. A&T scored six touchdowns, including a 31-yard sprint up the middle of the Eagles defense by McHenry Norman. (Courtesy of the *Afro-American*.)

Aggies Down State Eagles By 14-0 Score

By T. FRED ALLEN

DURHAM, N. C.—The A. and T. Bulldogs, of Greensboro, with a bone crushing running attack, trounced the N. C. College Eagles, 12 to 7 here before a large crowd of Turkey Day rooters.

Breaux returned to coach A&T in 1937, and NCC hired William Burghardt after the departure of Coach Adams. A&T extended its win streak to four straight games by defeating the Eagles 14-7. Allen Lynch starred at halfback for the Aggies. The *Norfolk Journal and Guide* misprinted the final score. (Courtesy of the *New Journal and Guide*.)

In 1938, A&T rolled to a 25-0 victory over NCC. Senior halfback and team captain Allen Lynch scored two touchdowns. The game headline from the *Norfolk Journal and Guide* salutes the outstanding play of Lynch, who was selected to the All-CIAA team for 1938. (Courtesy of the *New Journal and Guide*.)

Captain Lynch Ends Career With Glory

Aggies Outclass Ancient Rivals By Score of 25 to 0

ub Back Scores on Last Period

ass to Give Aggies 7 - 0 Victor

A&T's 7-0 win over NCC in 1939 was its sixth consecutive victory. Between 1934 and 1939, A&T outscored NCC 100-7. A former Iowa and Big Ten standout, Homer Harris was the new coach for A&T. A touchdown pass from A&T quarterback Eddie Moore to second-string end Duncan Dottin was the game's only score. A&T's defense pitched a shutout, which sealed the victory. (Courtesy of the *Afro-American*.)

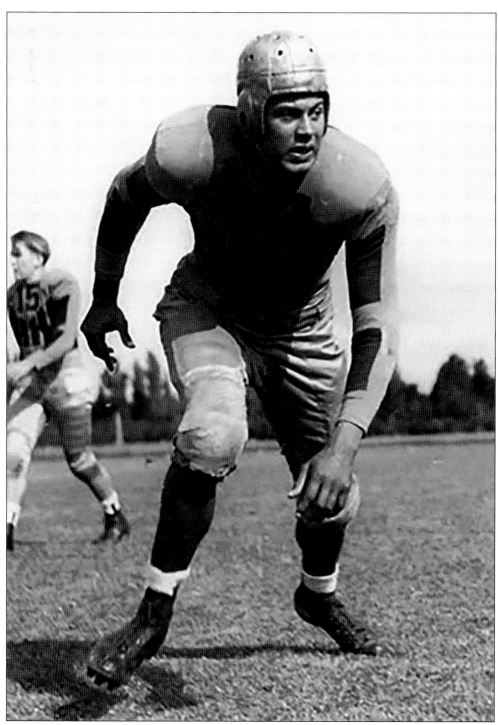

A native of Seattle, Washington, Dr. Homer Harris was named to the All-Big Ten team for three straight years at the University of Iowa. He was head coach at A&T from 1937 to 1938 and finished his short coaching career with a winning record. Harris later graduated from Meharry Medical School and set up a private practice in his hometown. (Courtesy of the *Seattle Times*.)

Two

REMEMBER THE TITANS
1940–1959

In many ways, 1940 to 1959 was a high watermark for the teams and the rivalry. Both teams had future Hall of Fame coaches and rosters with future professional players. Because of racial segregation, most of the best African American football players in North Carolina were on the rosters of NCC and A&T.

Before coming to NCC, coach Herman Riddick (1945–1964) won 82 games, lost 3, and tied 5 at Hillside High School in Durham. At NCC, he continued his success by becoming the winningest and longest-tenured coach in the school's history. His career record was 112-56-11, winning five CIAA titles (1953, 1954, 1956, 1961, and 1963) and one national title (1954).

William "Big Bill" Bell became head coach at A&T in 1946. Over the next 10 years, his Aggies won CIAA championships in 1950 and 1951 and the national title in 1951. Bert Piggott (1957–1967) replaced Bell as head coach in 1957. Piggott won the CIAA championship in 1958 and 1959.

Outstanding players filled the rosters of both teams in the 1940s and 1950s. "Big" John Brown from NCC and Robert "Stonewall" Jackson from A&T were pioneers in professional football. In 1947, Brown, a center, became the first African American player to sign with the Los Angeles Dons, a professional team in the short-lived All-America Football Conference (AAFC). In 1950, Jackson, a running back, became the first HBCU player drafted by an NFL team when the New York Giants selected him in the 16th round. He later coached football for NCC from 1968 to 1999. Some of NCC's standouts from the 1940s included future Raleigh mayor Clarence "Baby" Lightner, quarterback; "Dr." William Augustus "Gus" Gaine, tackle; and Carl Galbreath, quarterback. Some of A&T's standouts included Charlie Weaver, halfback; Earl Clarke, guard; Roy Gearing, end; Sam Bruce, back; and Leroy Childs, center.

Al Montgomery was one of NCC's most outstanding players in the 1950s. He was the first Eagles quarterback to win three CIAA titles. "Big" John Baker starred as a tackle for NCC, played 11 years in the NFL, and was a part of NFL history. Playing tackle for the Pittsburgh Steelers in 1964, Baker sacked legendary New York Giants quarterback Y.A. Tittle. After the sack, Tittle sat on his knees in the end zone, and a photographer captured one of the NFL's most iconic photographs. Other notable Eagles from this era include Butler "Blue Juice" Taylor, quarterback; Ed "Magic Eye" Hudson, quarterback; and Ernest "Ernie" Barnes, tackle. Barnes played professional football for several AFL teams in the 1960s before becoming an internationally renowned painter.

In the 1950s, A&T produced its slate of football stars. None was more sensational than quarterback William "Red" Jackson, who led the Aggies to their first Black College National Championship in 1951. J.D. Smith was a game-changing fullback for A&T before being drafted by the Chicago Bears in 1955. In 1956, the San Francisco 49ers claimed him off waivers, and Smith established himself as one of the league's most outstanding ball carriers. San Francisco drafted Bernie McQueen off the Aggies' 1958 CIAA title-winning team to play end. Another standout was quarterback Paul Swann, who led the Aggies in passing (1956, 1958, and 1959) and to CIAA titles (1958 and 1959).

North Carolina College for Negroes Football Squad—1940

Maroon
Jersey

No.	Name	Pos.	Weight	Height	Year	Home Town
—	Allen, Buford	E	179	6-3	1	Kansas, Kansas
22	Alston, Alex	E	187	6-2	4	Henderson, N. C
31	Bell, Edward	G	183	5-9	3	Newbern, N. C.
—	Bond, Styrone	T	202	6-0	2	Windsor, N. C.
—	Booth, James	QB	155	5-2	1	Chapel Hill, N. C.
25	Boozer, Amzi	T	167	6-1	1	Kansas, Kansas
16	Brown, Floyd	HB	150	5-10	1	Gary, Ind.
28	Brown, Ira	FB	150	5-8	2	Youngstown, O.
35	Brown, John	C	200	6-4	1	Gary, Ind.
21	Catlett, James	T	179	5-10	1	Evansville, Ind.
—	Collins, Monroe	FB	191	6-1	1	Kansas City, Mo.
19	Davis, Percy	T	192	6-1½	2	Chicago, Ill.
20	Duke, Robert	G	169	5-8	3	Lynchburg, Va.
—	Durrah, Russell	C	170	5-11	1	Durham, N. C.
14	Duckwilder, Vincent	HB	170	6-0	3	Roanoke, Va.
27	Fine, Leo	E	160	6-1	2	Kansas, Kan.
—	Funderburke, Horace	C	158	5-11	1	Durham, N. C.
38	Gains, William	T	215	6-1½	1	Mamaroneck, N. Y.
—	Garrett, Denison	T	185	6-1	4	Greenville Indust., N. C.
18	Green, Shade	HB	175	6-0	3	Durham, N. C.
24	Gwynn, Curtiss	G	182	6-0	1	Kansas, Kan.
42	Hall, William	HB	200	6-2	3	Raleigh, N. C.
26	Hardy, James	HB	160	5-7	1	Gary, Ind.
29	Harris, Clinton	HB	175	5-10	1	St. Louis, Mo.
23	Johnson, Harold	QB	155	5-6½	2	Peoria, Ill.
30	Kirksey, Henry	E	165	5-9	2	St. Louis, Mo.
34	Lewis, Ben	T	185	6-2½	2	Rocky Mount, N. C.
11	Lightner, Clarence	QB	155	5-9½	3	Raleigh, N. C.
40	Mack, George	C	167	6-0	3	Topeka, Kan.
36	Mack, Richard	FB	178	5-10	3	Topeka, Kan.
13	McFarlan, Leon	QB	156	5-8½	1	St. Louis, Mo.
33	Moore, Roy	E	185	6-3	3	Charlotte, N. C.
—	Nimo, Roswald	G	169	5-8	1	St. Louis, Mo.
41	Peerman, William	E	184	6-2	3	Monessen, Pa.
10	Perry, Lawrence	G	165	5-10	1	Durham, N. C.
—	Peace, Leonardo	E	162	6-1	1	Chapel Hill, N. C.
—	Robeson, Rudolph	T	186	6-1	1	Atkison, Kan.
32	Smith, Lee	E	180	6-5	3	Emporia, Kan.
17	Walker, Leonard	G	190	5-11	1	Chicago, Ill.
39	Walston, Woodrow	T	185	6-4	3	Pinetop, N. C.
—	Warmick, Walter	HB	164	5-8	3	Peoria, Ill.
37	Washington, Nathaniel	G	200	5-11	3	Roanoke, Va.
15	Williams, James	FB	180	5-10	3	Raleigh, N. C.

HOME GAMES

November 2................Shaw University
November 9 ....Florida A. & M.
November 16................Johnson C. Smith

Manager................Harold Colbert, Mt. Vernon, Ind.

In 1940, A&T relied on the outstanding play of Washington State natives Sam Bruce and Ave Perkins to down the Eagles 12-6 at World War Memorial Stadium in Greensboro. The victory was the seventh in a row for the Aggies. A&T head coach Homer Harris was a native of Washington and recruited the two standout players to A&T. On Thanksgiving Day before a crowd of 6,000 fans, NCC got on the board first when quarterback Harold Johnson, from Peoria, Illinois, passed to William Peerman for a seven-yard touchdown. William Augustus "Gus" Gaines missed the extra point for the Eagles. The Aggies responded immediately. Backup running backs George Brummell and William Brown carried the Aggies into striking distance, and Ave Perkins scored on a short run from inside the five-yard line, notching the game 6-6. A&T's final tally came on a six-yard pass from Roy Moore to Sam Bruce. The 1940 roster reveals the importance Dr. James Shepard placed on recruiting players from beyond North Carolina. Of the 43 players on the NCC roster, 24 were from the Midwest and Northeast. Sixteen players were from North Carolina, and four were from Durham. (Courtesy of North Carolina Central University Archives–James E. Shepard Memorial Library.)

NCC head coach William Franklin "Big Coach" Burghardt (left) and athletic director John "Little Coach" McLendon (right) are pictured here. Burghardt came to North Carolina College in 1937. He was a teammate of Pres. Ronald "Dutch" Reagan at Eureka College in the early 1930s. Burghardt played center, and Reagan played guard. They remained close friends for the rest of their lives. Burghardt convinced NCC president James E. Shepard to hire John McLendon, a legendary basketball coach and athletic director, who hired history-making coaches Herman Riddick in football and Leroy Walker in track and field. Burghardt earned a doctorate in education at New York University in 1950 and worked for many years as chairman of the departments of health and physical education at Morgan State University and Bowie State University. James Naismith, the inventor of basketball, mentored coach John McLendon, a basketball innovator. McLendon, a member of the Basketball Hall of Fame, created the fast break and the four corners, a strategy for maintaining a lead before the shot clock was implemented. He coached at NCC from 1940 to 1952, winning a Black College National Championship in 1941. He is also the first African American to be a head coach of a predominantly white school, Cleveland State University (1966), and a professional basketball team, the Denver Rockets of the American Basketball Association (1969). (Courtesy of North Carolina Central University Archives–James E. Shepard Memorial Library.)

Majorettes have long been a fixture in HBCU bands. These lovely ladies represented the Blue and Gold of North Carolina A&T State University around 1940. Majorettes were a popular attraction because of their skilled baton performance, high steps, and short skirts. The composition of this squad includes young ladies of different skin complexions, which was not the case in some HBCUs at this time but is indicative of the inclusive spirit of Aggie Pride. (Courtesy of North Carolina A&T State University Archives and Special Collections.)

In 1941, A&T and NCC played before 8,000 fans at O'Kelly Field in Durham. In the closing minutes, the NCC team defeated A&T 9-6 on a "Dr." Gus Gaines dropkick from the 20-yard line. The victory for the Eagles ended a seven-game losing streak in the rivalry against the Aggies and won NCC its first CIAA conference title. NCC's first score came after a 35-yard pass from Dick Mack to Rudolph Robeson down to the four-yard line. On the next play, Robeson carried it in for the Eagles. Head coach Rollie Bernard was new to A&T in 1941. After two periods of defensive dominance from both teams, A&T's Ave Perkins tied the game 6-6 on a short touchdown run. The game came down to Gaines's successful last-second kick. At the end of the season, Johnson C. Smith head coach E.L. Jackson protested to CIAA officials about the eligibility of NCC player Henry "Big Dog" Thomas. After investigating the accusation, a special CIAA committee found that NCC coaches were unaware Thomas had played the previous season for Lincoln University in Missouri. But the committee ruled Thomas ineligible because he had not sat out a season per conference rules. Consequently, the Eagles had to forfeit all the games that Thomas played, including the prized victory over A&T. They also had to relinquish the CIAA championship. Eagles alumnus Alexander Rivera covered the 1941 game for the *Norfolk Journal and Guide*. Rivera was an accomplished sportswriter and photojournalist who established the North Carolina College News Bureau in 1939. (Courtesy of the *New Journal and Guide*.)

STATISTICS

	A.&T.	N.C.C.
Yards gained rushing	142	98
Number of punts	10	10
Yards gained by punts	310	346
First downs	10	4
Passes attempted	10	9
Passes completed	3	3
Yards gained on passes	75	14
Passes intercepted by	3	4
Fumbles recovered by	1	2
Kicks blocked by	0	1

The lineups:

Pos.	A. & T. (6)	N. C. State (9)
L.E.	Gearing	Robinson
L.T.	Lynn	Gaines
L.G.	Woods	F. Brown
C.	Monteiro	G. Mack
R.G.	Clark	Gwenn
R.T.	Garvin	P. Davis
R.E.	Smith	R. Moore
Q.B.	Helme	Arbuckle
L.H.	Bruce	Duckwilder
R.H.	Doub	LaFayette
F.B.	Douglass	Hall

A. and T.	0	0	0	6—6
N. C. State	0	6	0	3—9

Substitutions: A. and T.—R. Lee. Bryant, Burney, Perkins, Jones. W. Lee, Harrington. Brown, Armour. Lawrence. Rowe and Hill: N. C. State—McFarland. R. Mack, Williams. Washington, Green. Boozer, Hardy. Bell, and Rich.

Officials: referee. F. A. Wiley; umpire, M. O. Robinson; headlinesman, H. S. Blue; and field judge, A. O. Walker.

The game statistics and the starting lineups for each team are in this article from the December 13, 1941, *Norfolk Journal and Guide*. (Courtesy of the *New Journal and Guide*.)

The William Burghardt–coached 1941 Eagles football team wore helmets with the famed wing decal. Star players and future star players littered the Eagles roster and included "Dr." William "Gus" Gaines, tackle; George "Mighty" Mack, center and captain; William "Ram" Hall, back; Vincent "Duck" Duckwilder, back; Roy "D.D." Moore, end; Curtis "Tonto" Gwynn, guard; Edwin "Bunny" Rich, end; Clarence "Buckle" Arbuckle, back; Clarence "Baby" Lightener, back; and six-foot, four-inch "Big" John Brown, center and future first HBCU player to play professional football. (Courtesy of Attorney Eric Montgomery.)

1941 Team

The 1942 game was played in World War Memorial Stadium in Greensboro in front of 12,000 fans. North Carolina College won the game 16-12. William Brown, Emmanuel Douglass, Grady Smith, and Roy Gearing, All-CIAA end, played well in the defeat for the Aggies. William Augustus "Gus" Gaines, an All-American tackle, starred for the Eagles by successfully making three dropkicks. Dropkicks require the kicker to drop the ball on the ground and then kick it off the bounce. In 1934, footballs were made more aerodynamic to improve passing, but the pointy ends made the drop kick more difficult because the football's bounce was more difficult to control. Thus Gaines's feat was that much more impressive. It was also Gaines's second consecutive game leading the Eagles over the Aggies. The full sports page from the *Norfolk Journal and Guide* for December 5, 1942, includes a photograph of "Dr." William "Gus" Gaines, who also kicked an extra point in the victory over rival A&T. Gaines was a New York native, but his mother's family was from Asheville, North Carolina. (Courtesy of the *New Journal and Guide*.)

A. & T. Claims N. C. Grid Title
And Wants Morgan For C.I.A.A.

By SMITH BARRIER,
Sports Editor Daily Record

CHARLES DeBERRY

GREENSBORO, N. C.,—(S N S) —Greensboro A. and T. College's football team, greatest in the school's history, has received two New Year's day bowl bids, but the Aggies want to turn them down for a better proposition suggested today by the Greensboro Record.

Once beaten in the CIAA the Aggies have their eyes on the conference championship. It is rightfully theirs, too, despite claims of Morgan college of Baltimore. Morgan State College cancelled its annual visit to Greensboro this year, and while unbeaten and unscored on, it has won only two CIAA games.

The A. and T. gridders want to plany the Morgan team here New Year's Day with the CIAA championship at stake—and since Morgan released the following statement this week, "On the basis of this record (five wins, no losses, 160 points, none for opponents) Morgan rightfully claims the mythical national championship,"—A. and T. questions that too.

The A. and T. Bulldogs received invitations today to the Vulcan Bowl in Atlanta and the Flower Bowl in Jacksonville, Fla. Last January 1 the locals trimmed Southern University of Louisiana in the Flower Bowl.

Such a record as Coach Charles DeBerry has this year makes the Aggies a post-season favorite. They have trimmed seven foes with single upset loss to Virginia State. They have tallied 230 points against 33 for the opposition. Stars have been Chas. Weaver, a slippery halfback and best ball-carrier the CIAA, and Roy Gearring an all American end according to all rival coaches. Gearring's defensive play and pass catching sparked the final victory over Camp Butner on December 4 by the score of 52-6.

It is this record which has won the two bowl invitations for Coach DeBerry's Bulldogs——but the players would still rather tangle with Morgan State in the game that should have been played in Greensboro anyway.

Because of World War II, NCC did not play football in 1943 or 1944. However, A&T did play. In 1943, the Charles U. DeBerry-coached Aggies posted a 7-1 regular season record, good enough to win the title as the best HBCU in the state of North Carolina. DeBerry was a member of the 1927 A&T team that won the school's first CIAA conference title. At the end of the season, a dispute arose over who was the CIAA conference champion. Morgan, which canceled its game with the Aggies, crowned itself mythical conference champion after going 5-0 and not giving up a score. A&T refused to recognize Morgan as champion because the Bears only played two conference opponents and dodged the Aggies. (Courtesy of the *Atlanta Daily World*.)

Brennan King Assumes DeBerry Post Aug. 21

GREENSBORO, N. C.—Brennan L. King, one of the greatest athletes ever graduated from A. and T. College, will take over the football coaching duties of the Aggies this fall, succeeding Charles U. DeBerry who has resigned.

Grid practices for the Aggies will begin September 5, and the nine-game schedule opens September 30 with the Winston-Salem Teachers playing at Memorial Stadium here.

King will be assisted by Karl M. Keyes, another former Aggie. Both assume their duties August 21.

SUCCESSFUL YEAR

DeBerry's resignation becomes effective August 21 at the

BRENNAN KING

end of summer school, and it is reported that he has under consideration several other coaching jobs. The popular coach had outstanding teams at his alma mater, last year rolling up nine victories against a single defeat to claim the co-championship of the CIAA with Morgan State.

King, holder of the B. S. degrees in physical education is a native of Seattle, Wash., and a graduate of the Garfield High School of that city. He is resigning the coachship of Dudley High School here to accept the position as athletic director of A. and T. College. King distinguished himself as a football player while in college, where he earned a regular end's berth on the varsity team.

CAROLINA NATIVE

Keyes, the assistant coach, is a native and graduate of New Bern's public schools. He received A. and T.'s B. S. degree in vocational agriculture here since that time. Keyes, too, made a fine record as a member of the varsity team during his college days.

Among the players of 1943 expected to return this fall are Charles Wenver, triple threat of Chapel Hill, and Chris Bryant of Raleigh, who ran 102 yards Thanksgiving to beat J. C. Smith University.

The Aggies' football schedule for the approaching season is as follows:

September 30—Winston-Salem Teachers College, here. October 7—Open; 14—Hampton at Hampton, Va.; 21—Open; 28—West Virginia State at Institute, W. Va. November 4 — Morgan State (homecoming) here; 11—Open; 18 —Virginia State, here; 30—Johnson C. Smith (Thanksgiving) here.

In 1944, NCA&T president Ferdinand D. Bluford hired Brennan L. King (pictured at right) to replace Charles DeBerry as head football coach and athletic director. By shutout victories, Coach King won his first three games as coach of the Aggies. To end the season, the Aggies played Texas College in the Flower Bowl in Jacksonville, Florida, but lost 18-0. Coach King was a former NCA&T basketball and football All-American during the tenure of coach Homer Harris. Both King and Harris were from Seattle, Washington. Harris also recruited Sam Bruce (pictured above) from Seattle to play for A&T beginning in 1938. Bruce was a star quarterback, and King was a star end. Bruce and King had hoped to coach together one day. However, in 1940, Bruce joined the Army Air Corps, and in 1942, he became a member of the 99th Pursuit Squadron or Tuskegee Airmen. During Operation Shingle in 1944, Sam Bruce gave his life in service to his country over Anzio Beach, Italy. (Above, courtesy of Find-a-Grave; right, courtesy of the *New Journal and Guide*.)

In 1945, the Eagles whipped the Aggies 40-0. It was coach Herman Riddick's first matchup against the Aggies and produced the largest victory margin for NCC in the history of the rivalry. Coach Riddick's charges played with precision from the T formation. Carl Galbreath of Fayetteville and Roy Lee of Durham scored a pair of touchdowns for the Eagles in the win. Pres. James E. Shepard at NCC hired Herman Harry Riddick away from Durham's Hillside High School in 1945. Riddick was the second Hornet coach Dr. Shepard brought to NCC. He hired Leo Townsend from Hillside in 1930. At Hillside, Riddick's teams won 82 games, lost 3, and were tied 5 times between 1936 and 1945. With 118 wins, 46 losses, and 12 ties, Riddick remains NCCU's all-time winningest football coach. Riddick, an All-CIAA performer, played receiver for the Eagles from 1930 to 1932. He was on the first NCC team to defeat NCA&T and never lost to the Aggies as a player. Riddick taught biology at NCC and was as popular as an instructor as a coach. (Courtesy of North Carolina Central University Archives–James E. Shepard Memorial Library.)

Bill Bell To A. And T. On February 1

BELL

NORFOLK—The fact that Bill Bell, the Army lieutenant who coached the Tuskegee Army Airfield eleven for the past two years, will arrive at A. and T. College, Greensboro, N. C., to assume his job as head athletic coach on or about February 1, was discovered by the Journal and Guide in an interesting fashion.

A note, written by Coach Bell, to the Journal and Guide circulation department said simply: "Effective as of February 1, kindly change the address on the subscription of Lt. William Bell, Tuskegee Army Airfield, Tuskegee, Ala., to William Bell, A. and T. College, Greensboro, N. C."

An alert circulation department clerk, Roderick Corprew, picked up the note and forwarded it to the news department which gives us the nearest thing to a definite analded arrival of Coach Bell to A. and T. College, which signed him to a coaching contract way last summer.

Coming off three straight losses, A&T upset previously undefeated NCC 17-0 at World War Memorial Stadium in 1946. Approximately 7,500 spectators watched the Aggies roll over the Eagles. It was the first game new A&T head coach Bill Bell coached in the rivalry. Muriel Reed scored on a short run for the Aggies in the first period of play. James Rowe kicked a nine-yard field goal in the second to give A&T a 10-0 lead at the half. Robert "Stonewall" Jackson, who later coached for over 30 years at NCCU, intercepted a pass on the NCC 45-yard line and raced for a touchdown and the game's final tally. A pride-filled Aggie defense contained coach Herman Riddick's Eagles all day. Because of Bill Bell's prior success, there was a lot of anticipation and excitement for his arrival at A&T in 1946. He did not disappoint. A&T's football team was floundering when he arrived. In 1945, the Aggies won only two games. "Big Bill" Bell was only 4-4 in 1946, but all that mattered to the Aggies in his first season was that he upset the undefeated and favored Eagles. (Courtesy of the *New Journal and Guide*.)

William McNeil "Big Bill" Bell was the first Black football player for The Ohio State University, suiting up for the Buckeyes from 1929 to 1932. He went on to have a stellar career as a college football coach. In 1949, legendary NCC basketball coach John McLendon wrote a prescient article for the *Carolina Times*, Durham's Black-owned newspaper, about NCA&T and "Big Bill" Bell. Coach McLendon, also athletic director at NCC, believed Coach Bell could help A&T achieve its enormous potential. McLendon wrote prophetically, "A. and T. is big! It is potentially, if not actually, the largest school in the CIAA. A. and T. not only in Athletics, but in many areas, has been a sleeping giant which, when fully aroused, will forge to the front to be challenged by all teams, with any idea of supremacy in any area." Bell proved McLendon correct, winning A&T's first Black College National Championship in 1951. In 1934, Claflin College wisely gave Bell his first head coaching job. Bell turned Claflin into a conference champion, and Florida Agricultural and Mechanical College (FAMC) took notice. In 1936, the Rattlers persuaded Bell to come to Tallahassee. Bell assembled an unsurpassed staff, including future legendary coach Alonzo Smith "Jake" Gaither. Under Bell's tutelage, FAMC became a juggernaut, winning conference titles in 1936, 1937, and 1942 and national titles in 1938 and 1942. Bell coached the Tuskegee Army Airfield (TAAF) team during World War II from 1943 to 1945. In November 1945, in front of 20,000 fans, TAAF defeated NCC 14-0 in the Capital Classic at Griffith Stadium in Washington, DC. Bert Piggott, who followed Bell as head coach of NCA&T, scored two touchdowns on long runs for TAAF. Before joining Bell's staff at A&T in 1949, Piggott was a teammate of NCC's "Big" John Brown on the Los Angeles Dons. (Courtesy of The Ohio State University Libraries.)

Cheerleaders are featured in the 1946 *Eagle* yearbook at North Carolina College. Pictured from left to right are Georgia Jones, Julius T. Glover, Vivian Austin, James D. Saddler, and Willie Hermenia Fitts. Hermenia Fitts was born in Warren County, North Carolina, in 1928 and graduated from North Carolina College in 1949. She attended graduate school in Atlanta, Georgia, and married Winslow Loring Jackson from Chicago, Illinois, a Harvard graduate. Jackson's father, Alexander Jackson, was a Harvard graduate, a founder of the Association for the Study of African American Life & History (ASALH), and a founder of the Chicago branch of the Urban League. (Courtesy of DigitalNC.org Yearbook Online Archive.)

TO DON DON GEAR—Latest pro football acquisition is John Brown, brilliant center of the 1946 North Carolina State College eleven, who was signed last week by the Los Angeles Dons of the All-America Football Conference, according to Don representative, Frank Clement. Brown, 6-foot, 2-inch, 235-pounder, is a product of Roosevelt High School, Gary, Ind., and twice made AFRO All-CIAA teams.

In October 1947, Dr. James E. Shepard, founder and president of NCC, died during the football season. Dr. Shepard supported the football program and actively participated in decisions about the team, including hiring head coach Herman Riddick. Undoubtedly inspired by Dr. Shepard's passing, Riddick and the Eagles blanked A&T 16-0. NCC jumped to an early lead, and A&T never recovered. NCC quarterback Thomas Allen completed a 30-yard pass to Willie Moore for the Eagles' first score. They missed the extra point. On the ensuing kickoff, A&T fumbled deep in its territory, and James Lineberger kicked a 21-yard field goal to give the Eagles an early 9-0 lead. Carl Galbreath scored for the Eagles on a two-yard run in the game's closing minutes. John Brown was an All-CIAA and All-American center for North Carolina College. Brown arrived at NCC in 1940, played for the Eagles through the 1942 season, and was a member of the 1941 team that initially won the CIAA conference title before an ineligible player caused the CIAA to forfeit several of their games. Brown served in the Army from 1943 through 1945 and was one of three Black football players in the military's Spaghetti Bowl, an all-star game played in Florence, Italy, in 1945. In 1946, Brown returned to NCC and played center for Herman Riddick's Eagles. He earned a spot on the *Chicago Defender* All-American and All-CIAA teams. At the end of the 1946 season, the Los Angeles Dons drafted Brown to play in the All-America Football Conference. Brown was one of the first African American professional football players. (Courtesy of the *Afro-American*.)

Robert Herman "Stonewall" Jackson, no. 34 (far right), is pictured with his New York Giants teammates. Jackson was one of NCA&T's best players in the 1940s and in 1950 became one of the first players from an HBCU drafted into the NFL. Born in the small town of Mineral, Virginia, in 1921, Jackson lived with his grandmother until 1932, when he moved to Allentown, Pennsylvania, to live with his parents. A three-sport star at Allentown High School, Jackson served in the US Army during World War II and was with General Patton and the Third Army when it crossed the Rhine into Germany in 1944. Jackson was awarded three Bronze Stars as a combat engineer in the all-Black 183rd Engineering Battalion. After the war, Jackson enrolled at NCA&T in 1946 and graduated in 1949. He played football from 1946 to 1948. After his three-year NFL career, Jackson earned a master's degree in physical education from Springfield College and took up coaching. After head coaching stints at Johnson C. Smith University and Shaw University, he joined coach George Quiett's staff at NCC in 1968 and remained at the institution for 31 years, retiring in 1999. Coach Jackson was a player favorite and is a member of the halls of fame at NCCU and NCA&T. (Courtesy of Attorney Eric Montgomery.)

Aggies' Late Rally Ties N.C. State College, 6-6

GREENSBORO, N.C. — A determined band of North Carolina A. and T. College Aggie fought off defeat here Saturday afternoon with a thrill-packed second half attack to gain a 6-6 deadlock with Coach Herman Riddick's North Carolina College Eagles from Durham in the final home game of the season.

The Aggies will start immediate preparations for the Vulcan Bowl game with the Kentucky State Thoroughbreds at Birmingham, New Year's Day.

After being outplayed by the Eagles during the first two periods, the Aggies showed a reversal of form in the latter stages to score once and threaten seriously two other times.

The Eagles tallied their marker in the second quarter when Bill Middleton, all-CIAA center from Charleston, S.C., intercepted the first attempted Aggie pass from Bill Jackson and raced 55 yards to cross the goal standing. James Lineberger attempted the placement.

Drive 58 Yards

The Aggies scored on a 58-yard march early in the fourth quarter, completing a series of passes that set the stage for Athie Garrison, triple-threat halfback from Canton, Ohio, to plunge over from the four-yard stripe for the touchdown. Garrison's attempted placement was blocked by James Elliott.

The battle was fought on almost even terms. The Eagles rang up nine first downs against eight for the Aggies. The Aggies netted 11 yds. from scrimmage against 95 for Eagles. The Eagles drew five penalties for 55 yards, one which nullified a touchdown, while the Aggies drew six penalties for 40 yards.

In the aerial department, the Aggies completed five of 12 attempted passes for 49 yards while the Eagles completed two of nine for 29 yards. The Eagles intercepted two passes, one which accounted for their touchdown, while the Aggies also intercepted two, running them back for 20 yards. Each team fumbled once on the muddy field with the Eagles recovering both times, once to block a determined Aggize drive.

In 1948, the Aggies and Eagles tied 6-6. In the second quarter, Bill Middleton, NCC center, picked off a pass from Bill Jackson and raced to the end zone for the game's first score. A&T halfback Athie Garrison scored from four yards out to tie the game in the fourth quarter. The point after attempts by both teams failed. The standouts for the game included Carl Galbreath from Fayetteville, North Carolina, for the Eagles and Hornsby Howell for A&T. Howell, who was head coach at A&T from 1968 to 1976, blocked a punt. The game was played at World War Memorial Stadium in Greensboro. (Courtesy of the *Afro-American*.)

In a game played at Durham Athletic Park, behind the stellar play of Marion Butler "Blue Juice" Taylor, NCC defeated the powerful Morgan State team by a score of 14-13. The Eagles' win was their first ever football victory over the Bears. (Courtesy of the *Afro-American*.)

As Eagles Whipped Bears for First Win in History

This power drive took place at Durham Athletic Park Saturday when the N.C. College Eagles defeated the deep-in-talent Morgan Bears, 14-13, for the first Eagle victory over the Bears in N.C. College history. The Eagles' wingback, "Blue-juice" Taylor, of Newport News, Va., races around right end with (left to right) Red Allen of Durham, Herman Hines of Wilson, and Willie Bradshaw of Durham running potent interference and blocking Morgan's end, Willie Harris, of Philly, to start the Bears' downfall.

In 1950, A&T quarterback William "Red" Jackson, master of the T formation, led the Aggies to a 25-13 victory over the Eagles and claimed the CIAA conference title for the first time since 1927. A&T scored 25 straight points before the Eagles got a single tally. Jackson, a former star at Parker-Gray High School in Alexandria, Virginia, threw two touchdowns and ran for another. The Eagles came alive in the fourth quarter, scoring twice, but it was too little too late. NCA&T's first CIAA championship in 23 years made it into the November 1950 *Philadelphia Tribune*. The team photograph reveals how much the game has changed, including jerseys with no numbers higher than 60, facemask-less helmets, and players much smaller than they are today. (Courtesy of North Carolina A&T State University Archives and Special Collections.)

Marion Butler "Blue Juice" Taylor Jr. played quarterback for NCC from 1948 through 1950. He is shown here with coach Herman Riddick. Taylor was an outstanding high school athlete and, in 1945, led Collis P. Huntington High School, a racially segregated school in Newport News, to the Virginia State Championship by scoring three touchdowns and passing for another. Taylor's best season at NCC was 1950, his final year, when he led the Eagles to a 6-0 conference record leading up to the Turkey Day Classic against the Aggies. A&T ended that perfect record. (Courtesy of Attorney Eric Montgomery.)

14,000 See A & T Aggies Win
Fourth Successive Carolina Classic

Wm. 'Red' Jackson, Six Other Varsity Heroes End Career

GREENSBORO, N. C.—A Durham junior tackle proved the undoing for the North Carolina College Eagles here last Thursday as Bill Bell's A. and T. College Aggies won the Carolina Classic, 13-6, before a crowd of holiday fans.

The victory break came in the last quarter with less than four minutes left in the ball game when Walter Hunter, All-American candidate, broke through to block McClellan Matthews' punt. Rube Phillips, freshman guard, fell on it in the end zone for the winning marker.

SCORE FIRST

The Eagles drew blood in the second quarter after capitalizing on a fumble by William "Red" Jackson on the Aggie 18. Fred James and Mel Spencer collaborated to move the ball to the two yard line. Joe Battle, Eagle quarterback, went over on a sneak to score. Matthews' extra point try was low.

The Aggies scored in the third quarter after Robert Jones, Aggie freshman defensive halfback, intercepted a Battle pass on the North Carolina Eagles' 43. Donald Quarles took a Jackson handoff and went 14 yards to the 29. Leroy Washington plunged to the 25 and Quarles took another handoff from Jackson and went the distance behind vicious blocking.

MATTHEWS' DRIVE

The game turning break came as Washington punted to the Eagle 12 and Battle returned to the 17. After two plays they were forced to kick when the Aggie forward wall had allowed them only one yard in two plays. Matthews went into punt formation on the third down and Hunter, 230 pound tackle, drove through with such force that when he blocked the punt it went into the end zone where Phillips fell on it. Jackson kicked the extra point.

BATTLE MAKES IT

The Durhamites took advantage of several first quarter breaks when after kicking off to the Aggies they forced their hosts to punt out from their own ten yard line. The Aggies began defensively on their own 48 yard line when Jerome Evans returned Washington's midfield punt. The Eagles pounced on this early opportunity and went down to the Aggie 15 yard line sparked by Spencer and James went nine and twelve yards respectively to place the ball on the Aggie two yard line. Battle went over through the center of the line for the first score of the game.

HOLD AIR ATTACK

The Eagles dominated the play of the first half with a net average of 96 yards from scrimmage to the Aggies' 52 but the Aggies managed to equal their visitors with four first downs each and nullified their passing game, allowing only one out of five.

The second chapter of this spectacular gridiron drama was all Aggie. On the ground the Aggies ran up 102 yards while holding the Eagles to a miserly 26. The Bellman completed two out of six passes but intercepted two of North Carolina's seven second half attempts.

LOSE HEROES

The game wrote finis to the careers of seven Aggies who have made a valuable contribution to the rise of football here under Coach Bell's administration. They are: William "Red" Jackson, Bill Blakely, Al Morgan, Helburn Meadows, Ira Snell, Robert Paul Smith, Cornelius Stephens, Leroy Washington, and Stanley Porter.

The victory over the vaunted Eagles boosted the Aggies' national prestige and removed the Eagles from the list of contenders in the CIAA and national picture.

Before playing NCCU in 1951, A&T handed perennial CIAA champion Morgan State its worse defeat in 22 years. NCA&T entered the home finale with the Eagles with a record of 5-1-1. Coach Herman Riddick's Eagles boasted a 7-0-1 record and had not given up more than seven points in any game. Three quarters of play proved the teams were evenly matched. The fourth quarter opened with the score tied 6-6. The deciding points came from a risky NCC punt attempt from its two-yard line. Aggie fullback John Paul Smith broke through the Eagle forward wall and blocked the kick. Aggie guard Reuben Phillips recovered the ball in the NCC end zone for a touchdown for the Aggies. William Blakely's point after was successful, making the score 13-6, which ended up being the final tally. A&T was led by Jack Gibson, William "Red" Jackson, Leroy Washington, and Donald Quarles, collectively known as "the Big Four." In addition to the Big Four, Helburn Meadows and Al Morgan starred for NCA&T. Quarterback Joe Battle, end Earnest "Ernie" Warlick, halfback Melvin Spencer, and fullback McClellan Matthews played well offensively for NCC. NCA&T star quarterback William "Red" Jackson and teammates Bill Blakely, Al Morgan, Helburn Meadows, Ira Snell, Robert Paul Smith, Cornelius Stephens, Leroy Washington, and Stanley Porter played in their final Carolina Classic in November 1951, having never lost to the Eagles. The victory was the third consecutive in the rivalry for the Aggies and knocked the undefeated Eagles from CIAA and national title contention. (Courtesy of *Philadelphia Tribune*.)

In 1951, NCA&T finished the season 7-1-1 and won its first Black College National Title. Coach Bill Bell called his aggregation the best team he fielded in 19 years of coaching. Bill Nunn, a sportswriter for the *Pittsburgh Courier*, named senior Aggies quarterback William "Red" Jackson to the *Courier*'s All-American team. NCA&T's outstanding backs for 1951 (pictured from left to right) Jack Gibson, William "Red" Jackson, Leroy Washington, and Donald Quarles spelled doom for Aggies opponents. (Courtesy of DigitalNC.org Yearbook Online Archive.)

THE NEWS BUREAU
NORTH CAROLINA COLLEGE
DURHAM, NORTH CAROLINA

THE CENTRAL INTERCOLLEGIATE ATHLETIC ASSOCIATION
OFFICIAL FOOTBALL SQUAD ROSTER
1953–1954

NAME	NO.	AGE	HEIGHT	WEIGHT	POSITION	CLASS	HOMETOWN
Aikens, Jack	81	19	5'8"	255	G	Soph.	Charlotte
Alexander, George	79	18	6'	175	B	Fresh.	Salisbury
Boone, Matthew	85	20	5'11"	235	T	Soph.	Hampton, Va.
Chambers, Samuel	68	24	5'10"	187	G	Junior	Chapel Hill
Crawford, James W.	69	22	6'	232	T	Soph.	Chapel Hill
Cunningham, Belton	63	19	6'1"	186	T	Fresh.	Charlotte
Darden, Cleveland	22		6'	187	B	Fresh.	Snow Hill
Davis, James	89	24	5'9"	175	C	Fresh.	Durham
Dockery, Zander		24	5'9"	170		Junior	Philadelphia, Pa.
Eason, Cornelius	76	20	5'7"	171	B	Junior	Norfolk, Va.
Edwards, Ralph		18	5'6"	162	B	Fresh.	Snow Hill
Evans, Jerome	71	22	5'9"	175	B	Junior	Goldsboro
Floyd, Charles	67	21	5'10"	167	E	Junior	Wilson
Garris, Roger	52	22	6'	186	G	Fresh.	Rich Square
Gerst, Lawrence	92	18	6'	170	E	Frosh.	Williamsburg, Va.
Glascoe, John T.		17	5'7"	153	B	Fresh.	Raleigh
Glenn, Charles	59	20	6'	222	G	Senior	Winston Salem
Harvey, Otto	95	25	5'10"	207	C	Junior	Elizabeth City
Hines, Ross	88	20	6'	194	E	Soph.	Detroit, Mich.
Herbert, James		20	5'10"	185	B	Fresh.	Springfield, Mass
Holley, Leon	65	19	5'7"	173	B	Fresh	Norfolk, Va.
Hollingsworth, William	77		6'1"	200	E	Senior	Goldsboro
Horton, Willie Cletis	93	23	5'11"	175	B	Junior	Charlotte
James, Robert	91	24	6'1"	209	C	Fresh	Kinston
James, Rudolph			5'5"	197	G	Soph	Hertford
Johnson, Linwood	72	23	5'11"	193	B	Senior	Elizabeth City
Jones, Linwood	61	23	5'11"	176	E	Senior	Norfolk, Va.
King, Henry	94	20	6'1"	175	B	Junior	Durham
Korngay, Harry		20	5'7"	227	G	Fresh.	Kinston
Lewis, Henry	90	19	6'2"	193	E	Fresh.	Williamsburg, Va.

In 1952, NCA&T came to Durham and throttled NCC 26-0 at Durham Athletic Park in front of 8,000 fans. A&T's victory ruined the Eagles' chances for a CIAA conference title. Otha Miller was a difference-maker for coach Bill Bell's Aggies. The first-year quarterback threw for two scores. The 26-0 victory pushed Coach Bell's record against coach Herman Riddick to 5-0-1. In 1953, on a cold and windy afternoon before 7,000 fans at World War Memorial Stadium in Greensboro, the NCC football team defeated NCA&T 15-6 for its first victory over A&T in seven years. Passing the ball only four times, NCC running backs Amos Thornton, Jerome Evans, and Linwood Johnson carried the Eagles to victory. A harbinger of the next three contests was the dynamic play of freshman quarterback Al Montgomery, who proved himself to be a capable field general. The win earned NCC its first CIAA championship. The Eagles went 6-1 on the season. This partial team roster for 1953 reveals that although most of the Eagles players were from North Carolina, there were players from as far away as Detroit, Michigan, and Springfield, Massachusetts. (Courtesy of North Carolina Central University Archives–James E. Shepard Memorial Library.)

Robert Albert "Al" Montgomery starred for the Eagles from 1953 to 1956. Montgomery was the first quarterback to lead the Eagles to a CIAA championship, ultimately winning three. Montgomery was from Gastonia, North Carolina, where he was a multisport star at Highland High School. His son, Atty. Eric Montgomery, played for the Eagles from 1983 to 1986. Both father and son are in the Alex M. Rivera Athletics Hall of Fame at NCCU. (Courtesy of Atty. Eric Montgomery.)

In 1954, NCC defeated A&T 7-6 on its way to winning its second consecutive CIAA championship and first Black College Football National Championship. Before a chilled home crowd of 11,000, NCC came from behind and scored in the fourth quarter to defeat the Aggies. A&T's score came in the second quarter when Henry Joseph recovered an Al Montgomery fumbled punt in the end zone. It was big news whenever the Aggies and Eagles clashed, as this November 1954 issue of the NCC *Campus Echo* student newspaper reveals. Students held multiple pep rallies during the week anticipating the big game. (Courtesy of North Carolina Central University Archives–James E. Shepard Memorial Library.)

Ed "Magic Eye" Hudson, a third-string quarterback from Williamsburg, Virginia, came into the game in the fourth quarter in 1954 and completed three consecutive passes for 38 yards, including a touchdown to sophomore flanker Henry "Hank" Lewis. Dearl Webster's successful point-after kick was the difference in the game. (Courtesy of Atty. Eric Montgomery.)

N. C. Marker In 4th Frame Ties Classic

Deadlock Is Aggies 3rd In A Row; TD's Go To Hawkins, Baker

GREENSBORO, N. C. — An underdog eleven for N. C. College pushed over a fourth period touchdown to deadlock the A. and T. College Aggies 7-7 in their Thanksgiving Day clambake, the 25th annual Carolina Football Classic here last Thursday afternoon at Memorial Stadium.

More than 7,500 fans from every nook and corner in the state were on hand for the usual event in which the unusual almost always hapens and saw A. and T. windup its campaign with its third deadlock in a row. Earlier the Aggies were tied by Fla. A. and M., 28-28 and Va. State 7-7.

• • •

In the 33rd year of the rivalry, A&T and NCC tied 7-7 at World War Memorial in front of 7,500 fans. A&T halfback Arthur Worthy scored on a short run off-tackle. Worthy set up the score for A&T when he intercepted Ed "Magic Eye" Hudson and returned it to the Eagles 22-yard line. NCC quarterback Al Montgomery got the underdog Eagles going in the fourth period when he completed a 22-yard pass to Durham halfback George Alexander, who was forced out at the nine-yard line. After a play that gained the Eagles five yards, "Big" John Baker, a former standout at Ligon High School in Raleigh, carried the ball into the end zone from the four-yard line. Coming into the game, A&T was 4-1-2, having tied its previous two contests. NCC was 4-1-1. A&T finished the season in second place in the CIAA. NCC came in fourth place. (Courtesy of the *New Journal and Guide*.)

49

In 1956, NCC shut out A&T 20-0 and won its third CIAA championship in four years. NCC's first score came on a trick play. The Eagles set up in field goal formation on the A&T 10-yard line. Al Montgomery received the snap, but rather than place the ball to be kicked, he pitched it back to kicker Dearl Webster, who passed to end Bobby Johnson. Johnson then ran the ball for a touchdown. On the next series, NCC's Francis Roberts intercepted A&T quarterback Otis Perry's pass and returned it for an Eagles touchdown. Cravis Bullock scored the final touchdown for the Eagles. Bullock, a Granville County native, took the handoff from Ed "Magic Eye" Hudson and eluded Aggies defenders for a 76-yard touchdown. NCC was undefeated in the regular season. A&T promoted Bert Piggott to head coach of the Aggies. Coach Bill Bell's record versus NCC was 5-4-2. NCC head coach Herman Riddick's (center) staff included James Stevens (left), Floyd Brown (behind Stevens), and James Younge (right). Stevens previously coached football, basketball, and track at Prairie View A&M. In 1965, Stevens replaced Riddick as head coach of the Eagles. Floyd Brown was an NCC alumnus and served as the head basketball coach, and James Younge had prior coaching experience at now-defunct Morristown College in Knoxville, Tennessee. He later became athletic director at NCCU. (Courtesy of Atty. Eric Montgomery.)

NCC was 1956 CIAA champions. Senior quarterback Albert Montgomery is at center in the first row (no. 53). Some other identified players include Charles Barron (no. 49), second from right in the first row; Albert Umstead, (no. 61), sixth from left in the second row (partially obscured); James Bryant (no. 88), fifth from left in the third row; and Ernie Barnes (no. 87), second from right in the fourth row. (Courtesy of Atty. Eric Montgomery.)

Freshman Eagles in 1956 included (from left to right) Albert "Red" Umstead, James Bryant, and Ernest "Ernie" Barnes. Umstead graduated from Hillside High School in 1952 and served in the military before earning a football scholarship at NCC in 1956. Ernest "Ernie" Barnes played professional football after NCC and became an internationally recognized artist. His 1976 painting *Sugar Shack* sold for $15.3 million in 2022. (Courtesy of Atty. Eric Montgomery.)

A 1956 photograph of the well-attired Aggies coaching staff includes William "Big Bill" Bell (seated at center) flanked by Mel Groomes to the left and Murray Neely to the right. Bert Piggott is standing behind Bell. Neely starred as a tackle for Bell when he coached at FAMC in the late 1930s. Neely also coached the track team at A&T. Melvin Groomes played football at Indiana. He coached the baseball team at A&T. Bert Piggott played football at the University of Illinois and under Coach Bell for the Army Airfield team at Tuskegee. (Courtesy of Atty. Eric Montgomery.)

CAROLINA CLASSIC

NORTH CAROLINA

A. & T. AGGIES

VS. 25¢

N. C. COLLEGE
EAGLES

THANKSGIVING DAY

THURSDAY, NOVEMBER 28, 1957

2:00 P. M.

GREENSBORO MEMORIAL STADIUM

In 1957, A&T thumped the Eagles 21-0 at World War Memorial Stadium in Greensboro. It was the first victory in the rivalry for new A&T head coach Bert Piggott and the first for the Aggies since 1952. Ed "Magic Eye" Hudson's interceptions set the Eagles back. Piggot called Aggies quarterback Howard Smith off the bench to lead his charges, and Smith bedeviled the Eagles all game with his passing and ball handling. Edward Godbolt intercepted NCC quarterback Ed Hudson's pass at the end of the first quarter and returned it to the Eagles 16-yard line. An NCC personal foul penalty moved the ball to the one-yard line. On the next play, at the beginning of the second quarter, A&T running back Charlie Davenport dove into the end zone for A&T's first score. Edward Nesbitt intercepted Hudson just before the half and returned it 34 yards for a touchdown. Howard Smith scored the final A&T touchdown on a short run around the right end. Pictured is a souvenir copy of the football program for the 1957 game. (Courtesy of Atty. Eric Montgomery.)

The Aggies were loaded with talent in the late 1950s. Pictured from left to right are James Toon, Bernie McQueen, and Johnny Wardlaw. They chat while getting dressed for a game. Toon played professionally in the Canadian league and coached Fayetteville State University's football team from 1997 to 1999. McQueen played his best football against NCC, and Wardlaw played in the Atlantic Coast Football Leagues, which served as a farm league for NFL and AFL teams. (Courtesy of Atty. Eric Montgomery.)

NCC football players (from left to right) Walter Browning, "Big" John Baker, Dearl "Toe" Webster, and Frank Roberts pose for a photograph. John Baker became a star at NCC. A graduate of Ligon High School in Raleigh, Baker played for the Los Angeles Rams, Philadelphia Eagles, Pittsburgh Steelers, and Detroit Lions after coming to NCC. He was elected the first African American sheriff of Wake County in 1978. "Toe" Webster was also a standout for the Eagles. (Courtesy of Atty. Eric Montgomery.)

In 1958, the game was played at O'Kelly Field, where the Eagles had not lost since 1953. Both teams were undefeated and untied on the season. But on this day, backup A&T quarterback Paul Swann doomed the Eagles. Swann connected with Joe Taylor in the first quarter on a 37-yard touchdown pass. Swan hooked up with Bernie McQueen on a 50-yard touchdown reception on the Aggies' next possession. Bernie Anderson scored the final touchdown for the Aggies on a short run. NCC answered in the second quarter when running back Pete Hayes scored a rushing touchdown. Ike "The Whip" Gatling scored on a one-yard run and had a passing touchdown to "Gorgeous" George Wallace that covered 64 yards. The play of Swann and a sluggish start doomed Riddick's men. The victory earned A&T the CIAA championship. The Aggies won the crown by defeating NCC 20-18 in Durham. Bernie McQueen (no. 80) takes in a pass for the Aggies and races for a long score. In the background, the Chidley Hall dorm is visible. (Courtesy of the North Carolina Collection Photographic Archives, the Wilson Library, University of North Carolina at Chapel Hill.)

NCC quarterback Ike "The Whip" Gatling is at the bottom of the pile. He scored a touchdown for the Eagles on a short run. Before the 1970s, HBCU fans dressed to impress for games. That is evident in this photograph. (Courtesy of the North Carolina Collection Photographic Archives, the Wilson Library, University of North Carolina at Chapel Hill.)

In 1958, NCC and NCA&T were at the top of the CIAA conference standings while playing in Durham. The game is always intense when the Aggies and Eagles play, but the intensity increases exponentially when the conference title is on the line. Demonstrative of that intensity is this pile-up of players on the goal line. (Courtesy of the North Carolina Collection Photographic Archives, the Wilson Library, University of North Carolina at Chapel Hill.)

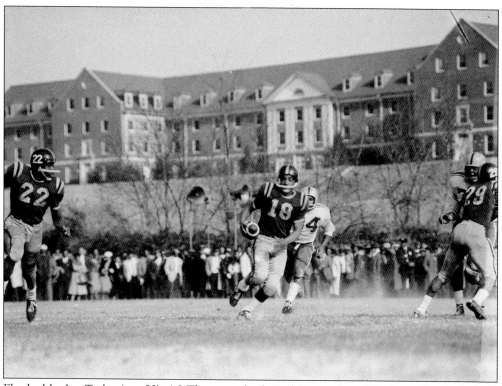

Flanked by Joe Taylor (no. 22), A&T's quarterback Paul Swann (no. 18) takes off with daylight in front of him. (Courtesy of the North Carolina Collection Photographic Archives, the Wilson Library, University of North Carolina at Chapel Hill.)

In 1959, in Greensboro, both defenses dominated. A&T did just enough to win. Over 8,000 spectators watched quarterback Paul Swann hold the ball for Eugene "Gene" Cambridge, who booted a 23-yard field goal with just two minutes left. The successful field goal ensured the Aggies a hard-fought 3-0 victory. Interestingly, Cambridge was the high school teammate of A&T running back Joe Taylor. Aggies referred to the two as the "Florida Ponies." A&T's victory over NCC gave the Aggies a 5-0-0 record and their second consecutive CIAA championship. (Courtesy of the *News and Observer.*)

A&T Wins Title

GREENSBORO (AP) — North Carolina A&T captured its second consecutive CIAA grid championship here Thursday by defeating North Carolina College, 3-0, on Eugene Cambridge's 25-yard field goal in the final period.

The victory game the Aggies a 5-0-0 CIAA record, good enough for the crown.

Lovely Aggies cheerleaders sporting bouffant hairstyles prepare for their next routine during a game in the late 1950s. (Courtesy of North Carolina A&T State University Archives and Special Collections.)

Three

AN ERA OF TRANSFORMATION AND CHANGE
1960–1979

The 1960–1979 era of the football rivalry coincided with the modern civil rights movement and the integration of higher education and collegiate football. Before the 1970s, most of the state's top African American high school football players played for A&T and NCC. With the acceleration of racial integration of many predominantly white universities, especially after 1970, these players increasingly attended historically white schools. In 1971, NCC and A&T left the CIAA and became charter members of the Mid-Eastern Athletic Conference (MEAC).

Between 1960 and 1974, NCC experienced its greatest success in the rivalry by winning 10 out of 15 games. But beginning in 1975, A&T turned the tables and won 4 out of the last 5 games of the era.

At NCC, Herman Riddick continued his winning ways in the 1960s. Talented players such as William "Bill" Hayes, Charles "Bobo" Hinton, Richard Wilkins, and Robert Currington helped the Eagles capture the CIAA title in 1961 and 1963, beating strong A&T teams led by Willie Ferguson and Cornell Gordon to end both seasons. Hayes had a phenomenal coaching career at Winston-Salem State University and A&T. Hinton played for multiple NFL teams.

James Stevens replaced Coach Riddick, who stepped down at the end of 1964. Stevens's teams defeated A&T in 1965 and 1966, and his record was 2-1 against A&T. For the 1966 game, played at Durham County Stadium, two freshmen Eagles players were stars of the game. Quarterback Herman Mathews dazzled the crowd with his running and passing, and wide receiver Julian Martin was named NCC's MVP for the game. George Quiett became NCC's head coach in 1968. Quiett coached one of NCC's most impressive teams in 1972. That season, Alexander Jones and Jefferson Inmon helped the Eagles overcome a very good A&T team to win the MEAC title. Inman rushed for 181 yards, the second-best rushing day for an Eagle. Jones and Inman were named MEAC Defensive Player of the Year and Offensive Player of the Year, respectively. Overall, Quiett went 3-1-1 against A&T. In 1973, Willie Smith became the first NCC coach to win a conference title in his first year. Smith won three out of five meetings with the Aggies. In 1978, Alvin Cauthorn set a school record when he passed for 339 yards against A&T. In 1979, Henry "Hank" Lattimore was named head coach.

Coach Bert Piggott continued his success from the 1950s into the 1960s for A&T by winning the CIAA title in 1964. Strong play by standouts Cornell Gordon, Ronald Francis, Willie Beasley, Luther Woodruff, Carl Stanford, and Clifton Matthews made the Aggies perennial contenders for the conference title. Civil rights leader and 1984 presidential candidate Rev. Jesse Jackson played quarterback for A&T and was a member of the 1964 title team. Piggott finished his career at A&T with 55 wins, three CIAA titles (1958, 1959, and 1964), and a 6-5 record against NCC. Piggott also coached Elvin Bethea. A defensive end, Bethea is the lone representative in the Pro Football Hall of Fame from the two schools.

In 1968, coach Hornsby Howell replaced Piggott, and on their way to winning their second national title, the Aggies defeated a one-loss Eagles team led by future NFL star Doug Wilkerson. Willie Pearson, Stanley Jacobs, and Merle Code (cornerback) carried the Aggies over the Eagles.

In 1975, Howell defeated NCC and won the MEAC behind the play of Ellsworth Turner, George Ragsdale, Walter Bennett, and Dexter Feaster. Ragsdale was interim coach for A&T for part of the 2008 season. Howell finished his career with 47 wins and a 2-6-1 record against NCC. Jim McKinley succeeded Howell in 1977 and won five in a row against NCC to close out the era for the Aggies.

Having won two straight CIAA titles and defeated the Eagles the previous three seasons, A&T came to Durham as the favorite to win the CIAA crown in 1960. But on this day, the overmatched Eagles refused to be denied. A testament to the Eagles' determination for victory is that NCC churned out 292 yards on the ground against a formidable Aggies defense anchored by Lorenzo "Big Ren" Stanford and Mel Richardson, while the Eagles' "Maroon Terror" defense, led by Nick Jeralds and Charles "Bobo" Hinton, held the Aggies to 100 yards on the ground and 109 through the air. Richard "Richie" Hicks, the NCC quarterback, scored the game-winning touchdown for the Eagles in the second quarter. Nick Jeralds and Robert Currington blocked an A&T extra point in the second quarter, which was the difference in the outcome, a 14-13 Eagles victory. Durham County Stadium was the site of the game for the first time. Jim Mitchell (no. 9), quarterback; Gene Cambridge (no. 29), halfback; Joe Taylor (no. 22), halfback; and Bernie Anderson (no. 48), fullback, comprised the Aggies backfield for 1960. Mitchell was the passing and offensive leader that year. Head coach Bert Piggott recruited Cambridge from Florida, a state well known for its football talent. Their talent as runners and their home state earned the Aggies backfield the cognomen "The Florida Ponies." (Courtesy of Atty. Eric Montgomery.)

These huge linemen were members of the 1960 NCA&T team. Pictured are Lorenzo "Big Ren" Stanford (no. 72), Mel Richardson (no. 71), Carl Stanford (no. 74), Willis McCleod (no. 78), and Pollard Stanford (no. 73). (Courtesy of Atty. Eric Montgomery.)

Rossie Barfield (no.33), Eagles running back, eludes Aggies defenders as teammates Lewis Woods (no. 88) and Reggie Pryor (no. 20) look on. Barfield was drafted in two professional sports. The Chicago Bears of the NFL and the San Francisco Giants in baseball drafted him. (Courtesy of the North Carolina Collection Photographic Archives, the Wilson Library, University of North Carolina at Chapel Hill.)

Fans and Eagles cheerleaders look on in Durham County Stadium as Aggies running back Gene Cambridge (no. 29) turns the corner on Eagles defenders Charlie "Ringo" Watkins (no. 51) and Rossie Barfield (no. 33). (Courtesy of the North Carolina Collection Photographic Archives, the Wilson Library, University of North Carolina at Chapel Hill.)

Joe Taylor (no. 22), A&T running back, follows his blockers, including Lorenzo "Big Ren" Stanford (no. 72), while Charlie Cox (no. 81), Eagles defender, pursues. Taylor and Gene Cambridge were high school teammates. (Courtesy of the North Carolina Collection Photographic Archives, the Wilson Library, University of North Carolina at Chapel Hill.)

1961 CIAA Champions

In 1961, coach Herman Riddick and the Eagles defeated A&T 13-0 and won their fourth CIAA championship. NCC's upset victory over undefeated A&T denied the Aggies the conference crown. A&T finished with a 5-1 conference record in second place in the CIAA that season. NCC finished the season with a 5-0-2 conference record. Pictured is the 1961 North Carolina College CIAA championship team. (Courtesy of Atty. Eric Montgomery.)

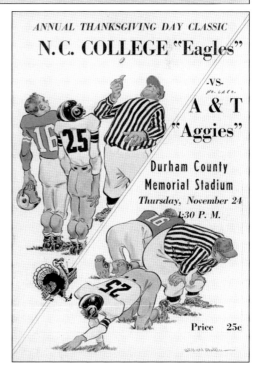

ANNUAL THANKSGIVING DAY CLASSIC

N. C. COLLEGE "Eagles"

-VS-

A & T "Aggies"

Durham County Memorial Stadium

Thursday, November 24
1:30 P. M.

Price   25c

This is the cover photograph from the program for the 1961 Thanksgiving Day Classic. Because of racial segregation and discrimination, white-owned printing services rarely depicted Blacks in football programs. Thus, the football cover photographs for the Thanksgiving Day Classic were generic during this period and before. (Courtesy of Atty. Eric Montgomery.)

63

Rev. Jesse Jackson was born in Greenville, South Carolina, in 1941 and attended Sterling High School. He was a star football player there and graduated in 1959. Jackson's football talent took him to the University of Illinois, but he transferred to A&T in 1961. A courageous leader with a strong moral compass, Jackson was a quarterback on the football team and student body president. He went on to establish Operation Push, run for president of the United States, and dedicate his life to social justice. Jackson (center, no. 48) and his teammates strategize. (Courtesy of North Carolina A&T State University Archives and Special Collections.)

Potent Ground And Air Attack Humbles Eagles

Matthews, Lee, Francis Tally Touchdowns As Aggies Notch Seventh Win In 9 Starts; Defeat Dips Riddickmen's Record To 6-3

A&T defeated NCC 28-7 at Durham County Stadium in a game the Aggies dominated on both sides of the ball. Aggies quarterback Jim Mitchell and halfbacks Willie Beasley and Clifton Matthews provided a potent rushing attack. Matthews accounted for two of A&T's touchdowns. His first touchdown came in the second quarter's opening minutes when he caught Mitchell's pass on the Eagles' eight-yard line, eluded NCC defenders, and scored. Center and linebacker William "Bill" Hayes partially blocked an A&T punt, which gave NCC the ball on A&T's 31-yard line. NCC quarterback Donald Thomas completed a pass to Charlie Cox down to the three-yard line. NCC's Bobby Asmond carried the ball for a touchdown two plays later. After the extra point, the score was tied at 7. Unfortunately for NCC, those were their only points on the day. At the beginning of the second half, A&T drove 75 yards in 18 plays. Matthews scored his second touchdown on a four-yard run. Aggies quarterback Cornell Gordon completed a 15-yard touchdown pass to Roland Francis early in the fourth quarter. Fullback Augusta Lee closed out the scoring for A&T with a four-yard touchdown run in the final minutes. This is the game headline from the December 1, 1962, *Norfolk Journal and Guide*. (Courtesy of the *New Journal and Guide*.)

COACH RIDDICK'S LAST CHAMPIONSHIP TEAM, 1963

For the almost 10,000 fans who attended in Greensboro, the 1963 game was a defensive showcase that ended with a 6-0 NCC victory. The win also earned NCC the CIAA championship, its second title in three years. Unintimidated by A&T's home-field advantage, NCC quarterback Aaron Martin led the Eagles on an 80-yard scoring drive in the first quarter. NCC then relied on its bend-but-don't-break defense to contain the Aggies. Martin started the scoring drive with a 56-yard completion to halfback Robert "Pedro" Currington, a former standout at Hillside High School in Durham. After a short gain down to the 24-yard line, Martin connected with Robert "Bob" Evans for a touchdown. NCC punter Billy Shropshire forced A&T to start drives deep in its territory. Shropshire averaged 40.4 yards per punt. One of his punts went for 51 yards. Statistically, A&T won the game. A&T had 13 first downs to NCC's 4. A&T had 135 rushing yards compared to NCC's 36, and the Aggies led in total yards: 219 to 166. But the box score favored the Eagles, who also led the Aggies in passing yards, 131 to 83. Currington was named MVP for the Eagles, and quarterback Cornell Gordon won that distinction for A&T. This photograph from the *Eagle* yearbook includes an inset photograph taken immediately following the team's victory. The 1963 CIAA championship was the last for coach Herman Riddick. (Courtesy of Edwin Jones.)

Played before 10,000 fans at Durham County Stadium, A&T defeated NCC 26-0 and won the CIAA championship in 1964. It was also Herman Riddick's final game as NCC's head coach in the rivalry. The combination of quarterback Cornell Gordon, Willie Beasley, and Ron Francis was too much for the Eagles. Beasley and Francis scored two touchdowns. Gordon passed to Francis early in the first quarter for an 82-yard touchdown. Willie Beasley scored on an 11-yard run in the second quarter. Gordon connected with Francis for a six-yard touchdown later in the second quarter. A&T had a commanding 19-0 lead at halftime. Beasley ended the scoring on a one-yard plunge to start the final quarter. Gordon was named MVP for A&T, while Staley Keith was NCC's MVP. Riddick's record against A&T was 8-10-2. John Baker starred for the "Little Blues" of Ligon High School in Raleigh, North Carolina, before playing tackle for NCC from 1954 through 1957. As a defensive end for the Pittsburgh Steelers, Baker sacked New York Giants quarterback Y.A. Tittle (no. 14) in 1964, causing him to throw an interception that his Steelers teammate Chuck "Bobo" Hinton, a former Ligon and NCC teammate and star, picked off and ran for a touchdown. That sack left Tittle, a future Hall of Famer, bruised and bloodied and was captured in an iconic photograph. (Courtesy of the *Mercury News*.)

In this 1964 photograph, as Cornell Gordon (no. 11), captain and starting quarterback of the Aggies football team, looks on, Bill Hayes, captain of the Eagles football team, and a game official look to the NCC bench to see if the Eagles will kick or receive the kickoff. (Courtesy of DigitalNC.org Yearbook Online Archive.)

In 1965, James Alexander "Coach Steve" Stevens won his first game in the rivalry as head coach of NCC. Coach Steve began working as an assistant football coach at NCC in 1954 after spending 1952–1953 on "Big" Bill Bell's staff at A&T. Neither team came into the game with title hopes as in years past, but a win would have secured a winning season for the Aggies. But instead, the underdog Eagles managed to pull the upset, giving coach Bert Piggott his first losing season as A&T's head coach. NCC scored in the first quarter on a six-yard run by halfback James Devone, a former Hornet from Hillside High School in Durham. Key plays on that drive were two 20-yard passes from Eagle quarterback Fred Baldwin to Charles Holloway and James McCleod. That was all the offense NCC could muster for the game because A&T's defense was so stout. It limited the Eagles to a net 35 yards of offense on the day. Particularly impressive for the Aggies were defensive tackles Elvin Bethea, William Sinclair, and Clyde Pettiway. A&T scored on a 10-yard touchdown run by Melvin Phillips, but John Grainger overthrew the extra point attempt. The Aggies finished the season 4-6, and the Eagles finished with a record of 3-5-1. NCC punter Billy Shropshire won the MVP award for the 1965 contest, which NCC won 7-6 over NCA&T. (Courtesy of Edwin Jones.)

In this 1965 photograph, coach Herman Riddick hands the ball off to coach James Stevens, symbolizing the end of an era in NCC football history. In 1965, Coach Riddick stepped down as the all-time winningest football coach at NCC, and Coach Stevens took over as head coach. (Courtesy of North Carolina Central University Archives–James E. Shepard Memorial Library.)

NCC and A&T played at the Durham County Stadium in 1966, and 10,000 fans were expected to attend. The Eagles won 12-6. NCC got on the scoreboard first with a one-yard run by quarterback Herman Matthews. Matthews scored after a short completion to running back Colin Oliver. Oliver is the father of current NCCU head coach Trei Oliver. A&T's lone score came on a short Craig Sills pass to Mike Johnson. A fourth-quarter interception by Stanley "Mighty Mouse" Gibbs was pivotal. Gibbs returned the interception to the A&T two-yard line. From there, NCC quarterback Walter Funderburk tossed the game-winning touchdown to senior receiver Roosevelt Robinson. Because Robinson was double-covered most of the game, freshman Eagle receiver Julian "Pete" Martin got most of the opportunities and was named MVP for NCC. Ollis Carson, Roy Anderson, and Colin Oliver, all running backs, also played well for the Eagles. A&T tackle Elvin Bethea won MVP for the Aggies. Bethea was credited with numerous bone-crushing hits and recovered two fumbles. Bethea is the only player from either school to be inducted into the Pro Football Hall of Fame. Halfback Willie Vaughn, defensive end Henry Hipps, and Mike Johnson also played well for the Aggies. In this photograph, NCC wide receiver Julian "Pete" Martin faces off with A&T's Carlton Oates (no. 46). Aggie players Warren Frye (no. 71), Bob Edwards (no. 63) Merle Code (no. 11), and Fred Battle (no. 74) pursue Martin. Eagles Lonnie Page (no. 75) and Colon Oliver (no. 38) race to assist Martin. (Courtesy of the North Carolina Collection Photographic Archives, the Wilson Library, University of North Carolina at Chapel Hill.)

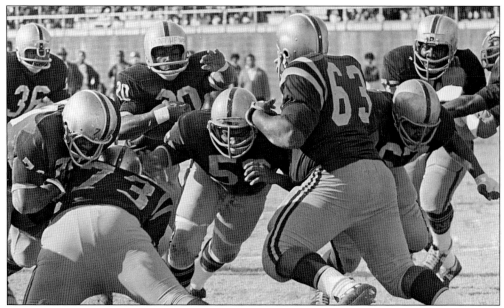

NCC quarterback Herman Mathews (no. 20) attempts a quarterback sneak at the Aggies goal line. Offensive linemen Sam Singletary (no. 70), Ervin Allen (no. 53), Harold Beatty (no. 67), and Lonnie Page (no. 75) block a wall of determined Aggie defenders that includes Bob Edwards (no. 63), Jerry McCollough (no. 73), and Fred Battle (no. 74). Running back Ben Carrington (no. 36) follows behind Mathews. (Courtesy of the North Carolina Collection Photographic Archives, the Wilson Library, University of North Carolina at Chapel Hill.)

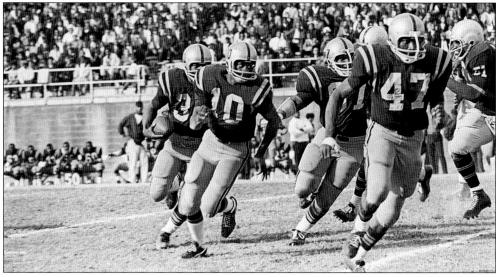

Hall of Fame Green Bay Packers head coach Vince Lombardi made the power sweep running play famous, but no team in HBCU football ran the power sweep with more precision and determination than the Aggies of North Carolina A&T State University. Every team on the Aggies' schedule had to prepare for it, including NCC. Here, A&T running back Willie Vaughn (no. 32) gets in behind a wall of Aggie blockers that includes Richard Armstrong (no. 47), Craig Sills (no. 10), and Gilbert Shelton (no. 67). (Courtesy of the North Carolina Collection Photographic Archives, the Wilson Library, University of North Carolina at Chapel Hill.)

Following the determined blocking of Craig Sills (no. 10) and Gilbert Shelton (no. 67), Aggie running back Willie Vaughn (no. 32) prepares to put his cleats into the ground as he turns the corner on the Eagles. NCC players Harold Beatty (no. 67), partially obscured, and James Smith (no. 51) give chase. (Courtesy of the North Carolina Collection Photographic Archives, the Wilson Library, University of North Carolina at Chapel Hill.)

Attorney H.M. "Mickey" Michaux (center), an alumnus of NCC who later became the longest-serving representative in the North Carolina Legislature, holds a game trophy after NCC defeated NC A&T 12-6 in 1966. Also pictured are Colon Oliver (no. 38) (left), running back and father of current NCC coach Trei Oliver; behind Michaux, Roosevelt Robinson (no. 82), end; Herman "Tweety" Byrd (no. 74), co-captain and second-team All-CIAA; head coach James Stevens (right); Edwin "Ed" Jones (no. 68), All-CIAA guard; and Louis Bell (no. 83), All-CIAA defensive end. (Courtesy of Edwin Jones.)

In Carolina Classic

Pearson Paces Aggies' 19-6 Win Over NCC

Willie Pearson was a one-man wrecking crew for the Aggies in the 1967 matchup between the longtime rivals, scoring all of A&T's touchdowns. Pearson, normally a halfback, was pressed into duty as a quarterback because of an injury to Merl Code and scored three times. NCC scored first. Quarterback Herman Matthews completed a 10-yard scoring strike to halfback Gilbert Smith to complete a 44-yard drive. From then on, seniors Elvin Bethea and Dennis Homesley led the Aggies defense in pitching a shutout. Pearson's first score came in the second quarter on a 10-yard run. After the Aggies stopped the Eagles to start the third quarter, Pearson returned the Eagles punt 91 yards for a touchdown. His final score came in the final quarter with Code in the game as quarterback. Code tossed a pass to Pearson from NCC's 17-yard line, and he eluded Eagles defenders for a touchdown. The final score was A&T 19 and NCC 6. (Courtesy of the *New Journal and Guide*.)

In 1968, George Quiett took over for James Stevens at NCC, and Hornsby Howell replaced Bert Piggott at A&T. Both new coaches proved outstanding for their respective schools and entered the game with identical 7-1 records. But it was Coach Howell who got off to the fastest start. Howell and his angry Aggies took out a talented NCC team 21-6 at Durham County Stadium on their way to winning the school's second national title. Howell's improbable national title in his first season overshadowed that CIAA pollsters placed the Aggies second in the CIAA standings behind Morgan State. When the Aggies declawed the Bears during the regular season, they were undefeated and had not lost in 31 games. Hornsby Howell played center for A&T from 1946 to 1949. He was All-CIAA and an All-American his senior year. Howell began coaching at Jordan Sellars High School in Burlington, North Carolina, in 1950. He was an assistant at Southern University in 1961 before joining Bert Piggott's staff the following year. Howell won a national championship in 1968 and a share of the MEAC title in 1975. He was 2-6-1 versus NCCU. (Courtesy of Atty. Eric Montgomery.)

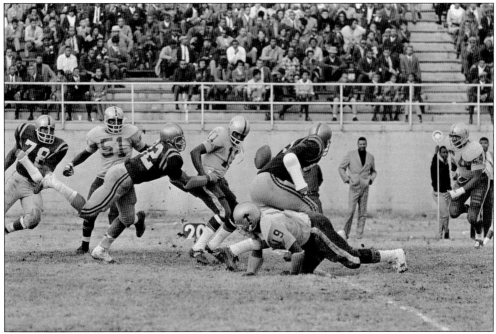

Wendell Bartee (no. 22), an A&T defender, strips the ball from the Eagles quarterback. (Courtesy of the North Carolina Collection Photographic Archives, the Wilson Library, University of North Carolina at Chapel Hill.)

Aggie running back Richard Armstrong (no. 32), who later played for the Kansas City Chiefs in the NFL, runs for daylight as teammate Darryl Cherry (no. 30) delivers a block that opens a gaping hole in the Eagles defensive front. Melvin Holmes (no. 73) looks on for the Aggies. Holmes's son Brad played for coach Bill Hayes at NCA&T, and in 2021 he became the executive vice president and general manager for the Detroit Lions. Eagle tackle Doug Wilkerson (no. 63) closes in on Armstrong. (Courtesy of the North Carolina Collection Photographic Archives, the Wilson Library, University of North Carolina at Chapel Hill.)

Doug Wilkerson (no. 63) and several Eagles are pursuing Darryl Cherry (no. 30). In 1968, Wilkerson was named to the American Football Coaches Association All-America team. Members of the A&T football team and the bandstand are in the background. (Courtesy of the North Carolina Collection Photographic Archives, the Wilson Library, University of North Carolina at Chapel Hill.)

In 1969, NCC became North Carolina Central University. Going into the game that season, Central and A&T had identical 7-1 records, and the CIAA title rested on the game. Quarterback Stan Jacobs and receiver Willie Wright gave A&T a commanding lead it maintained until late in the second half. Down by 22 with nine minutes left in the fourth quarter, the high-flying Eagles roared back behind quarterback Herman Matthews and receiver Julian "Pete" Martin, who combined for three touchdowns, and the game ended 28-28, enough to earn the Eagles an invitation to the Boardwalk Bowl to play the University of Delaware, the first time an HBCU and a predominantly white institution met in a bowl game. Delaware won 31-13. It was the final game the Eagles played as a member of the CIAA for a decade. Ollie Carson, Doug Wilkerson, Sam Singletary, Pete Quinn, Jerome Gantt, and Ervin Allen also starred for Central. Gene Harrison and Tommy Blue made significant contributions for the Aggies. (Courtesy of Atty. Eric Montgomery.)

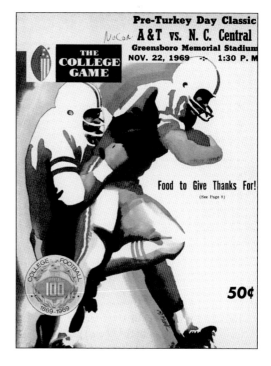

In 1970, NCCU defeated A&T 13-7 in Durham. Eagles quarterback Garvin Stone threw two first-half touchdowns to Jason Caldwell. Jerome Turner, Aggies quarterback, scored A&T's lone touchdown on a short run. NCCU finished the season 5-4, and A&T ended the season 4-6. Members of the NCCU Eagles marching band entertain fans from the stands. (Courtesy of the North Carolina Collection Photographic Archives, the Wilson Library, University of North Carolina at Chapel Hill.)

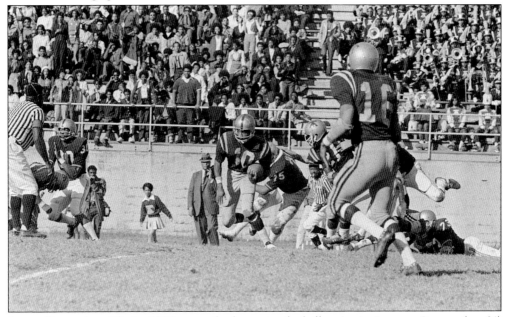

Jerome Turner (no. 10), the A&T quarterback, carries the ball as Aggies Lorenzo Pearson (no. 21) and Chucky Middleton (no. 16) look on. (Courtesy of the North Carolina Collection Photographic Archives, the Wilson Library, University of North Carolina at Chapel Hill.)

NCCU defensive coach Henry C. "Hank" Lattimore instructs the Eagles on the sidelines. In 1979, Lattimore became head coach at NCCU. When he stepped down in 1990, Lattimore was the second all-time winningest coach at NCCU. (Courtesy of the North Carolina Collection Photographic Archives, the Wilson Library, University of North Carolina at Chapel Hill.)

Garvin Stone (no. 16) watches as NCCU fullback James Smith (no. 36) follows Eagles blockers into a palisade of Aggies defenders, including Eddie Favors (no. 64). A&T's band and majorettes can be seen in the background. (Courtesy of the North Carolina Collection Photographic Archives, the Wilson Library, University of North Carolina at Chapel Hill.)

Aggies Yield To NCC TD Drive In Closing Minute

GREENSBORO, N.C. — At the beginning of the football game between A. And T. and N.C. Central last Saturday a fan stated that coaching would be the difference in the game.

And N.C. Central's Coach George Quiett decided to let his team go for first downs on fourth down situations with six minutes left in the final quarter and his Eagles behind 13-8.

THE GAMBLE paid off four consecutive times after Central began its winning drive at its 24-yard line. With powerful runners in James Smith and Jeff Inmon plowing for yardage every four plays, the Aggies could not stop the visitors scoring march.

Then with less than a minute to play and the Eagles situated on the Aggies' 22-yard line, Quarterback Garvin Stone let loose a high pass to tight end Jason Caldwell which the tall receiver hauled in on a leaping grab between two Aggie defenders.

THE EXTRA point was no good but Central had come from a one time third quarter deficit of 13-2 to win the game in the final minute, 14-13.

Except for a safety which put Central ahead early in the first quarter of the game, A. And T. came on strong to maul their visitors in the first half.

Following the safety, the Aggies recovered a Central fumble at the Eagle 44 and drove to the 32 on gallant running by AJ Holland and Robert Moore.

ON FOURTH down, Quarterback Leonard Reliford threw a 32-yard touchdown strike to Willie Wright and the Aggies were out front, 7-2.

In the second quarter, A. And T. struck again when Reliford hit flanker Charles Middleton beautifully on a 20-yard strike widened the gap to 13-2.

THEN CENTRAL got its running game together in the fourth quarter following a fumble by the Aggies' Robert Moore at his own 34.

The Eagles advanced to A. And T.'s 30 from where Stone hit running back Inmon on a 30-yard scoring pass that made the count, 13-8.

THEN WITH less than seven minutes left in the game Central got the ball after Dwight Nettles' second unsuccessful field goal try at their own 20. From there Coach Quiett decided to take all four plays, no matter what the risks, in order to catch up.

His gamble worked and the Eagles are now in a position to be considered for the Boardwalk Bowl in Atlantic City, N.J., Dec 4.

The 1971 game was played at World War Memorial Stadium in Greensboro, and for the first time, NCCU and A&T competed in football as members of the newly formed Mid-Eastern Athletic Conference (MEAC). NCCU forced an A&T safety early in the game, but on the next A&T possession, quarterback Leonard Reliford found flanker Willie Wright open for a touchdown that gave the Aggies an early 7-2 lead. In the second quarter, Reliford tossed a touchdown pass to Charles "Chucky" Middleton, giving the Aggies a commanding 13-2 lead. The Eagles came alive in the fourth quarter behind the play of Garvin "Che Che" Stone and the running of James Smith and Jefferson Inmon. Early in the fourth quarter, Stone hit Inmon on a touchdown pass that made the score 13-8 in favor of the Aggies. With eight minutes left in the game and more than 80 yards to cover, NCCU coach George Quiett decided to gamble and go for it on four consecutive fourth-down plays. Smith and Inmon converted the four fourth downs, and Stone passed to tight end Jason Caldwell for the game-winning score. A&T finished the season 6-4-1, and NCCU finished with a record of 7-2. The *Norfolk Journal and Guide* provided coverage of the rivalry from the 1920s into the new millennium. However, as desegregation increased, Black media outlets increasingly focused on African American athletes at predominantly white institutions. Also, in the 1970s, the white press began to cover Black sports more consistently, including HBCU football, which cut into what had been an almost exclusive market for the Black press before 1960. (Courtesy of the *New Journal and Guide*.)

In 1972, the Eagles and Aggies played at Wallace Wade Stadium at Duke University. The teams entered with identical 8-1 records and a chance to win the MEAC. Jefferson Inmon opened the scoring when he took a handoff, broke through the Aggies line, and raced 78 yards for a touchdown, but the Eagles missed the extra point. A&T answered when Leonard Reliford found George Ragsdale open on a short pass "Rags" took 77 yards to the house. With the extra point converted, A&T had a 7-6 lead. In the second half, Garvin Stone entered the game. Stone's play made the difference for the Eagles. With 5:35 left in the fourth, the Eagles took possession on their nine-yard line. Stone guided the Eagles to the Aggies 33-yard line, and with only 30 seconds remaining, freshman kicker Owen Williams entered the game. Williams had missed a 40-yard field goal and an extra point earlier, but when it mattered most, he delivered. His field goal gave Central a hard-fought 9-7 victory, the school's first MEAC title, and entry into the Pelican Bowl to play the Southwestern Athletic Conference (SWAC) champion. Coach George Quiett is from East Baton Rouge, Louisiana. He was educated at Shaw University, where he played football and basketball. The World War II veteran was an innovator—his 1972 offense placed a record nine players on the MEAC All-Conference Team. (Courtesy of North Carolina Central University Archives–James E. Shepard Memorial Library.)

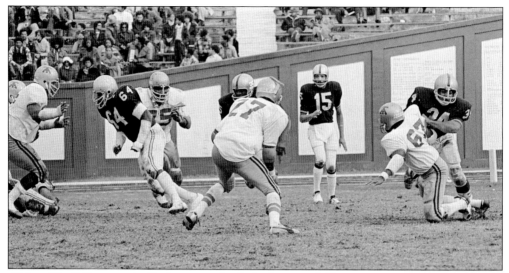

Clifton "Pop" Herring, the Eagles quarterback, looks on as Jefferson Inmon (no. 35) follows the blocking of Raymond Coleman (no. 64) and Herman Anderson (no. 34). William Wideman (no. 75), John Hampton (no. 27), and Donald Barnes (no. 67) attempt to make the stop for A&T. Herring later became the head basketball coach at Wilmington Laney High School, where he coached Michael Jordan. Herring allegedly cut Jordan from the team as a 10th grader. Herring later explained that he placed Jordan on the junior varsity team as a 10th grader so that Jordan could develop different aspects of his game. (Courtesy of the North Carolina Collection Photographic Archives, the Wilson Library, University of North Carolina at Chapel Hill.)

On his way to a 78-yard touchdown run, Jefferson Inmon (no. 35) breaks through the Aggies forward wall behind the blocking of Gordon Armstrong (no. 72) and Thomas Saxon (no. 60). Aggies defender Osceola "Sonny" Hicks (no. 9) pursues Inmon. (Courtesy of the North Carolina Collection Photographic Archives, the Wilson Library, University of North Carolina at Chapel Hill.)

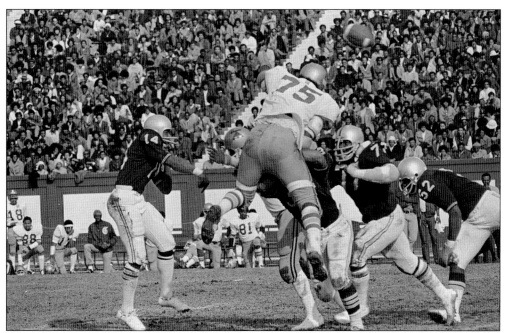

Jefferson Inmon (no. 35) and Darius Helton (no. 77) attempt to block A&T defensive end William Wideman (no. 75), who shows off his athleticism with a leaping deflection of Kenneth Wells's (no. 14) pass attempt. (Courtesy of the North Carolina Collection Photographic Archives, the Wilson Library, University of North Carolina at Chapel Hill.)

In front of a large crowd, Aggies offensive linemen Arthur Brown (no. 63) and Dan Coleman (no. 72) watch A&T quarterback Leonard Reliford pass to Alfred Holland (no. 33). David Plummer (no. 51) for the Eagles is in coverage. John Barbee (no. 65), Eagles and All-MEAC defensive tackle, came close to sacking Reliford. NCCU's Tony Townsend (no. 22) tracks the ball in flight. (Courtesy of the North Carolina Collection Photographic Archives, the Wilson Library, University of North Carolina at Chapel Hill.)

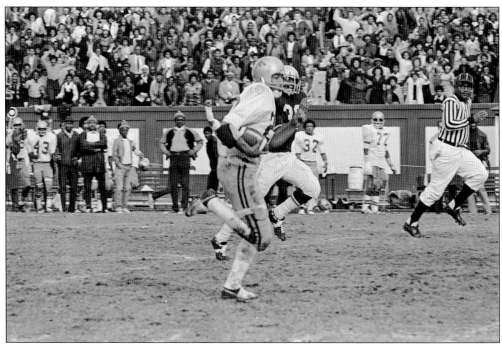

A&T running back George Ragsdale (no. 20) outraces Alexander Geno Jones (no. 38), MEAC Defensive Player of the Year for 1972, for a 77-yard Aggies touchdown. (Courtesy of the North Carolina Collection Photographic Archives, the Wilson Library, University of North Carolina at Chapel Hill.)

In 1973, the Eagles defeated A&T 16-6 and clinched the MEAC championship for the second year. Nearly 14,000 fans packed Memorial Stadium in Greensboro to watch the contest. Halfback James Smith scored both Eagles touchdowns. NCCU's Maroon Terror defense was in full force, not giving up a score until the final period and picking off quarterback Paul McKibbons four times. Clifton "Pop" Herring started at quarterback for the Eagles. He completed three passes on the day. Smith did most of the heavy lifting, rushing for 151 yards on 33 carries. Smith's first touchdown came in the opening quarter. He took a handoff from Herring and raced 45 yards for the score. In the second quarter, Tyrone Boykins kicked a 25-yard field goal to give the Eagles a 10-0 lead. Smith scored on a two-yard run in the third quarter, making the score 16-0. A&T finally got on the scoreboard in the fourth quarter on a short McKibbons touchdown run. NCCU blocked the point after. In 1973, Willie Smith (left) took over as head coach of the Eagles, replacing George Quiett, who stepped down for personal reasons. Smith had previously coached at Maryland Eastern Shore (1971–1972) and Norfolk State University (1967). He and Quiett were neighbors in the Emorywood subdivision. (Courtesy of North Carolina Central University Archives–James E. Shepard Memorial Library.)

The 1973 MEAC champion Eagles pose at O'Kelly Stadium. The team placed five members on the All-MEAC Defensive Team and nine on the All-MEAC Offensive Team. NCCU's Alexander Jones was Conference Defensive MVP, and Jefferson Inmon was Offensive MVP. (Courtesy of DigitalNC.org Yearbook Online Archive.)

The beautiful NCCU Majorettes for 1973 include (from left to right) Gloria Muldrow, Linda Fisher, Glenda Fisher, June Williams Michaux (head), Sylvia White, Angela Mills, Willie Darcell Mills, and Clarissa Lipscomb. (Courtesy of DigitalNC.org Yearbook Online Archive.)

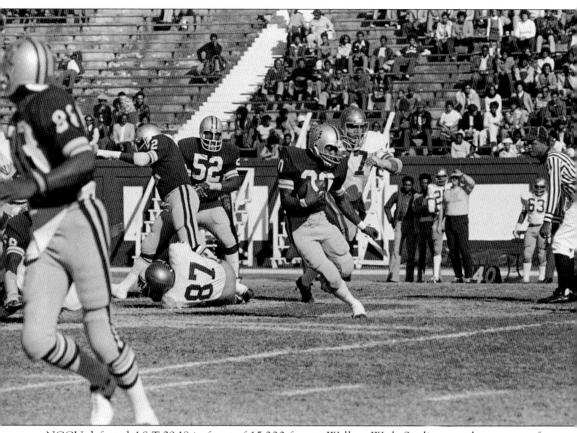

NCCU defeated A&T 29-18 in front of 15,000 fans at Wallace Wade Stadium on the campus of Duke University in 1974. Quarterback Ricky Moore contributed to all the Eagles' touchdowns. Moore opened the scoring less than three minutes into the first quarter with a one-yard dive for a touchdown. At the 9:29 mark of the first period, Moore connected with Terry Baldwin on a 12-yard touchdown pass. A&T struck back when George Ragsdale took the kickoff inside the Eagles 40-yard line. After Ragsdale was ejected for fighting, A&T quarterback Ellsworth Turner rallied the Aggies offense and guided them to their first touchdown, a one-yard Turner plunge into the endzone. Moore answered the Aggies' score with another Eagles touchdown, tossing a 64-yard strike to James Walls. At the half, the score was NCCU 20 and A&T 9. Because NCCU knocked Ellsworth Turner out of the game with a dislocated shoulder, quarterback Steven Ryan took Turner's place and guided A&T to a field goal in the third quarter. Moore answered the Aggies again by leading the Eagles on a 63-yard scoring drive. The touchdown came on a six-yard pass from Moore to Jim Alton. Jerome Boykin missed the extra point but later connected on a 25-yard field goal to end the scoring for NCCU. Ryan tossed a 26-yard touchdown to Herb McKinney to close out the scoring. NCCU running back Eugene Carmichael (no. 30) cuts in the open field and heads for daylight. (Courtesy of the North Carolina Collection Photographic Archives, the Wilson Library, University of North Carolina at Chapel Hill.)

A&T head coach Hornsby Howell looks on as his defense teams up to bring down the Eagle ball carrier. (Courtesy of the North Carolina Collection Photographic Archives, the Wilson Library, University of North Carolina at Chapel Hill.)

Fans watch in anticipation as Edwin Baldwin (no. 88) tracks the ball in flight and then outraces Aggie defenders for a long touchdown reception. (Courtesy of the North Carolina Collection Photographic Archives, the Wilson Library, University of North Carolina at Chapel Hill.)

An A&T defenseman wraps up Eugene Carmichael (no. 30). (Courtesy of the North Carolina Collection Photographic Archives, the Wilson Library, University of North Carolina at Chapel Hill.)

A&T Wins, Shares Title

N.C. A&T 34, N.C. Central 16 —
In this big rivalry at Greensboro, the Aggies turned it on, scoring all of their touchdowns before Central scratched, rolling up 408 yards total offense and upping their over-all record to 8-3. A&T finished 5-1 in the Mid-East Athletic Conference, tying S.C. State for first place.

A&T soundly defeated NCCU in 1975, ending a drought that stretched back to 1968. The final score was A&T 34 and NCCU 16. Memorial Stadium in Greensboro was the site of the contest, and 20,000 fans were in attendance. Early Eagles turnovers got A&T off to a fast start. After an NCCU fumble and an Aggie drive to the Eagles' one-yard line, star running back George "Rags" Ragsdale dove in to put A&T on the scoreboard first. Ellsworth Turner kicked the extra point. In the next series, Eugene Carmichael fumbled for NCCU. Turner made the Eagles pay for their mistake when he connected with Ron Scott on a short screen pass. Scott eluded Eagles defenders for A&T's second touchdown. After a long drive, Larry Barham scored the next Aggies touchdown on a six-yard run. NCCU answered when quarterback Rickie Moore guided the Eagles on a 62-yard drive that Delacio Bartley caped with a seven-yard touchdown run. Aggies running back Glenn Holland put the finishing touches on a 76-yard drive with a three-yard touchdown run. In the next series, A&T fumbled in its territory, and Moore got the Eagles on the board with a nine-yard quarterback keeper. A&T led 27-16 at the half. The second half was a defensive battle, and the Aggies shut the Eagles out. Ragsdale put the Aggies on his back on the final scoring drive, which covered 72 yards. "Rags" caught a 43-yard pass and scored on a two-yard run. A&T rolled up 408 yards of total offense. In 1975, A&T won its first MEAC championship. (Courtesy of the *Charlotte Observer*.)

An Aggie favorite, George "Rags" Ragsdale (no. 23) was a star halfback from 1972 to 1975. The Tampa Bay Buccaneers drafted him in 1976, but because of an injury, he did not get to play until 1977. He played a supporting role as a running back and kick returner for three seasons. Ragsdale was an assistant coach at A&T from 2003 to 2008 and interim head coach for part of the 2008 season. His son Marcus played for A&T in the mid-1990s. (Courtesy of Fandom.com.)

In 1976, NCCU came from behind to defeat A&T 17-16 in the final seconds of the game played at O'Kelly Stadium. During the game, A&T quarterback Ellsworth Turner became the first MEAC quarterback to pass for 2,000 yards. But Charles Armwood made the difference in the game. He completed five passes in a row to move the Eagles from their 42 to the Aggies' 15. From there, Eric Hines booted a 32-yard field goal to lift the Eagles over the Aggies. A&T standouts included Dexter Feaster, Ron Scott, Bruce Black, Calvin Hawkins, Glenn Holland, and Turner. Making an impact for NCCU were Reggie Smith, Maurice Bassett, Armwood, and Hines. A large crowd watches Ellsworth "Tookey" Turner (no. 10) fire a pass to an Aggie teammate, while Eagle defensive end Tyrone Boykin (no. 85) closes in. At the conclusion of his collegiate football career, Turner was a MEAC Champion quarterback, three-time All MEAC selection, conference Player of the Year (1976), and A&T's all-time leading passer. (Courtesy of the North Carolina Collection Photographic Archives, The Wilson Library, University of North Carolina at Chapel Hill.)

NCCU's Walter Odom (no. 50) has his eyes on Aggies running back Glenn Holland (no. 20) as he races for the hole in the Eagles forward wall. (Courtesy of the North Carolina Collection Photographic Archives, the Wilson Library, University of North Carolina at Chapel Hill.)

Ellsworth Turner (no. 10) watches running back Ron Scott (no. 34) elude Eagles defenders Louis Breeden (no. 34, far left), Joseph "Boogie" Ballard (no. 79), Bobby Miller (no. 71), and Walter Odom (no. 50) behind the blocking of Ron Aiken (no. 51) and Greg Roberts (no. 79). (Courtesy of the North Carolina Collection Photographic Archives, the Wilson Library, University of North Carolina at Chapel Hill.)

Eagle cheerleaders turn around to watch A&T running back Glenn Holland (no. 20) as he races around the left side of the Aggies line with Eagles defenders Reggie Little (no. 27) and Walter Odom (no. 50) in pursuit. James Brockington (no. 48) looks on from the Eagles sideline. (Courtesy of the North Carolina Collection Photographic Archives, the Wilson Library, University of North Carolina at Chapel Hill.)

Whenever A&T and NCCU play, a large crowd gathers, and the 1976 game at NCCU was no exception. Here the crowd and team have erupted in celebration. In the photograph are NCCU head coach Willie Smith, to the right of Maurice Bassett (no. 84); long-time assistant coach Robert "Stonewall" Jackson to the left of Reginald "Super Gnat" Smith (no. 21); assistant coach James Carter to the right of Smith; and to the right are Wilbert Simpson (no. 83), Leroy Jordan (no. 80), and Thomas Lancaster (no. 28). Between Lancaster and Tyrone Boykin (no. 86) is Dallas "Little Dal" Simmons, who played basketball at NCCU in the 1980s. (Courtesy of the North Carolina Collection Photographic Archives, the Wilson Library, University of North Carolina at Chapel Hill.)

In 1977, Jim McKinley replaced Hornsby Howell as head coach at A&T, and the Aggies thumped the Eagles 25-6 at Memorial Stadium in Greensboro. A&T's defense played lights out all game, and the offense got rolling in the second quarter when record-setting quarterback Ellsworth Turner dished a short screen pass to Lon Turner, who followed blockers 52 yards to paydirt. In the next sequence, Tony Currie intercepted a Charles Armwood pass and returned it to the one-yard line. A&T halfback Glenn Holland carried it over from there. NCCU fumbled the ball at its 25-yard line before the half, and Currie recovered. After a 20-yard completion to Frank Carr, Ellsworth Turner ran it in from the five-yard line. The score was A&T 22 and NCCU 0 at the half. After the half, the Aggies added a field goal, and Jim Lawrence scored a touchdown for NCCU. In 2007, James Ruffin "Jim" McKinley (left) received the Distinguished Alumni Award from Western Michigan University (WMU), where he played tight end from 1963 to 1965. He is pictured with WMU president John M. Dunn. McKinley coached A&T until 1981 and ended NCCU's run of victories. NCCU went 11-5-1 against A&T between 1960 and 1976. McKinley came to A&T from Central State in Ohio. He is the only Aggies coach to defeat NCCU twice in the same season, 1980, and he had a 5-1 record against NCCU. (Courtesy of MLive.com.)

A&T back Lon Harris (no. 40) fights for yardage against the Eagles. The photograph is from the *Register*. (Courtesy of North Carolina A&T State University Archives and Special Collections.)

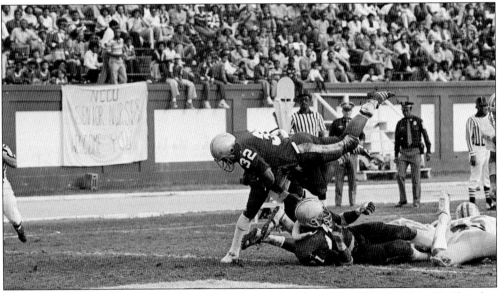

A&T traveled to Durham in 1978 and came from behind to defeat NCCU 17 to 13. Played at Wallace Wade Stadium at Duke University in front of 18,000 spectators, the game stars were Alvin Cauthorn for NCCU and Charles Sutton for A&T. Cauthron set a rivalry record by throwing for 339 yards. Sutton rushed for 243 yards and two fourth-quarter touchdowns. His second score sealed the victory for A&T. Ray Green coached the Eagles for the 1978 season. Anthony Judd (no. 32) demonstrates Eagle Pride with a giant leap over A&T's defensive line for a Central touchdown. (Courtesy of the North Carolina Collection Photographic Archives, the Wilson Library, University of North Carolina at Chapel Hill.)

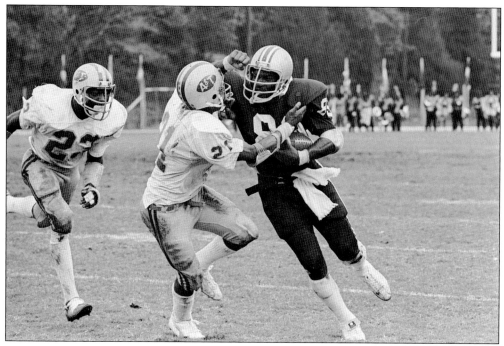

NCCU receiver Joe Mack (no. 89) fights for yardage as Aggies defenders converge to stop him. (Courtesy of the North Carolina Collection Photographic Archives, the Wilson Library, University of North Carolina at Chapel Hill.)

Aggies offensive players create a clean pocket as A&T's quarterback drops back to pass. (Courtesy of the North Carolina Collection Photographic Archives, the Wilson Library, University of North Carolina at Chapel Hill.)

NCCU quarterback Alvin Cauthorn (no. 14) rolls out as Aggies defenders look on. (Courtesy of the North Carolina Collection Photographic Archives, the Wilson Library, University of North Carolina at Chapel Hill.)

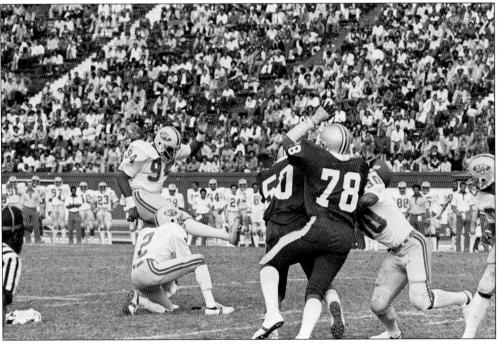

The Aggies attempt a field goal as the Eagles' Walter Odom (no. 50) and Randal Evans (no. 78) close in. (Courtesy of the North Carolina Collection Photographic Archives, the Wilson Library, University of North Carolina at Chapel Hill.)

	NCCU	NC A&T
First Downs	15	18
Rushes-Yds	48-161	59-223
Passing Yds	104	109
Return Yds	4	-68
Passes	6-19-1	5-14-1
Punts-Avg.	9-43.8	7-36.7
Fumbles-Lost	2-1	6-3

N.C. Central	0	13	7	0—20
N.C. A&T	14	6	0	3—23

A&T— Sutton 14 run (James kick)
A&T— Davis 37 pass from Myers (James kick)
NCC— Burnette 1 run (Birth kick)
A&T— Sutton 1 run (kick failed)
NCC— Peak 20 pass from Pugh (kick failed)
NCC— Burnette 1 run (Birth kick)
A&T— James 18 FG

INDIVIDUAL STATISTICS

RUSHING — NCC: Burnette 20-88, Pugh 15-36, Hamilton 6-25, McIver 5-9, Tillery 2-3; **A&T:** Pitts 37-196, Sutton 7-18, C.Johnson 5-13, Feggie 2-1, Myers 8-(-5).

PASSING — NCC: Pugh 5-13-1-80-1 tdp, Yuille 1-6-0-24; **A&T:** Myers 5-14-1-109-1 tdp.

RECEIVING — NCC: Peak 3-65, Sanders 2-29, Foster 1-10; **A&T:** Davis 2-48, Harris 1-38, Carr 1-18, Mimms 1-5.

In 1979, Henry "Hank" Lattimore replaced Ray Green at the helm for the Eagles. In another hard-fought game at Memorial Stadium in Greensboro, A&T defeated NCCU 23-20 with an 18-yard Keith James field goal in the closing seconds. A&T jumped to a 14-point lead. The second score came on a 37-yard touchdown pass from Roland Myers to Oliver Davis. NCCU fought back with a touchdown on a short run by Robert Burnette. Charlie Sutton, who scored A&T's first touchdown, scored again, making the score 20-7. A touchdown pass from NCCU quarterback Kenny Pugh to Greg Peak before the half cut A&T's lead to 7 points. The Eagles defense stiffened in the second half, and the offense tied the game in the third quarter, but James's field goal closed it out for A&T. This game box score is from the November 18, 1979, *Durham Morning Herald*. It reveals that the teams were evenly matched except for rushing yards and fumbles. A&T won despite fumbling six times. (Courtesy of the *Durham Morning Herald*.)

Four

THE ERA OF RECORD SETTERS
1980–1999

During the 1980s and 1990s, the rivalry between the Aggies and Eagles peaked, resulting in numerous record-breaking moments on the field. NCCU left the MEAC in 1980 and returned to the CIAA, which was a lower level. Division I-AA schools could provide 75 football scholarships, while Division II institutions were limited to 40, giving A&T an edge in talent due to the additional scholarships. The Aggie-Eagle Classic occurred at Carter Finley Stadium in Raleigh in the 1990s.

Coach Jim McKinley brought the Aggies into the 1980s with an impressive 9-3 record in 1980. A&T defeated NCCU in the regular season and the postseason Gold Bowl IV, which pitted the best team in the CIAA against the best team in the MEAC. Wayman Pitts, Frankie Chesson, and Billy Mims were named to the 1980 MEAC All-Conference teams, with Mims and fellow Aggie Mike West being named Sheridan Broadcasting Network All-Americans. McKinley was named MEAC Coach of the Year.

At the same time, NCCU coach Lattimore's offense became more explosive with players like quarterbacks Gerald Fraylon, Earl "Air" Harvey, and record-setting wide receivers Victor Hunter and Robert Clark. Fraylon finished his career with 5,794 passing yards. Harvey set 15 Division II passing records and a series single-game passing record against A&T in 1985 when he threw for 360 yards. Victor Hunter led the team in receptions in 1981 and 1982, while Clark set the career record for NCCU for most receiving yards (4,231).

Under Coach Lattimore's leadership from 1979 to 1990, NCCU won 77 games while losing 55. He was 5-8-1 against A&T and finished his career as the second longest-tenured coach in Eagles history.

In 1988, former NCCU player William "Bill" Hayes took over from Mo Forte, who had coached the Aggies from 1982 to 1987. Forte won the MEAC in 1986 and was named the MEAC Coach of the Year. Hayes took the Aggies to a new level, with 106 wins at A&T, three MEAC titles (1991, 1992, and 1999), and two national championships (1990 and 1999). Hayes is the winningest coach in the long and distinguished history of the rivalry and holds the record for consecutive victories. Hayes went 12-2 and won 12 straight over his alma mater. He retired from coaching in 2003. Some of Hayes's All-MEAC players included quarterback Connell Maynor, who in 2020 won a national championship as head coach of Alabama A&M; defensive back Alonzo Barnett; and running back Maurice Smith. Kevin Wilson, head coach at the University of Tulsa, was a member of Hayes's staff at A&T in 1988.

Former NFL great Larry Little headed NCCU's football team from 1993 to 1998, compiling a record of 33-32. Under Little, players like Monte' Southerland, who holds the record for most single-game, season, and career kickoff return yards, came to prominence. In 1996, the Eagles led the nation in pass defense amongst all NCAA Division II schools, with defensive backs Michael Wall, Chris Thompson, Buddy Crutchfield, Trei Oliver, Travis Sadler, and Adrian Jones leading the defense. Trei Oliver is the current head coach of the Eagles.

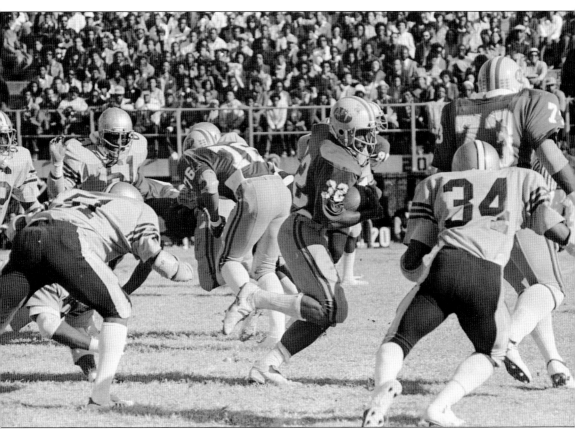

NCCU and A&T played twice in 1980, and the Aggies won both contests. The first game was played at NCCU. In the postseason, the teams played in the Gold Bowl IV in Richmond, Virginia. The game featured the conference champions of the MEAC and the CIAA. In 1980, A&T represented the MEAC, and NCCU represented the CIAA. A&T won decisively, 37-0. Aggies quarterback William Watson was named the game's most valuable player. He rushed for a touchdown and threw for another. Running back Cleotis Johnson also played well for the Aggies. He rushed for 112 yards and a touchdown. With Eagles in pursuit, A&T running back Cleotis Johnson (no. 32) follows the blocks of Thomas Boone (no. 76) and Bruce McAllister (no. 73). (Courtesy of the North Carolina Collection Photographic Archives, the Wilson Library, University of North Carolina at Chapel Hill.)

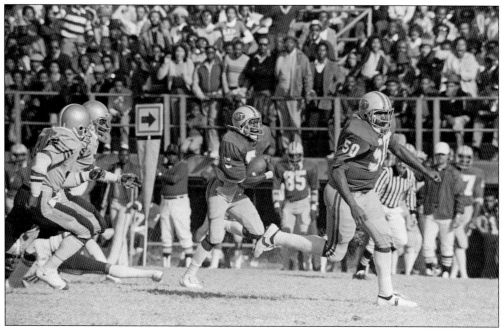

Big Donald Spicely (no. 50) leads the way for A&T quarterback Ronald Myers (no. 5). (Courtesy of the North Carolina Collection Photographic Archives, the Wilson Library, University of North Carolina at Chapel Hill.)

Ron Meyers (no. 5), Aggies quarterback, looks to pass the ball to Frank Carr (no. 25), A&T wide receiver, while teammate and offensive lineman Clifton "Big Smooth" Britt (no. 64) protects his back. (Courtesy of the North Carolina Collection Photographic Archives, the Wilson Library, University of North Carolina at Chapel Hill.)

An Eagles defender (no. 34) delivers a big hit on Aggies running back Wayman Pitts (no. 20). (Courtesy of the North Carolina Collection Photographic Archives, the Wilson Library, University of North Carolina at Chapel Hill.)

Central quarterback Charles Yuille (no. 11) hands off to running back Benjamin "Ben" Tate (no. 44) whiles Aggie defensive lineman Gerry Green (no. 93) and linebacker Frankie Chesson (no. 23) prepare to make a play. (Courtesy of the North Carolina Collection Photographic Archives, the Wilson Library, University of North Carolina at Chapel Hill.)

N.C. Central 35, N.C. A&T 7

— Clifton Kersey and Gerald Fraylon ran for two touchdowns each and Benny Tate rushed for 131 yards and another touchdown for the Eagles.

Kersey, who gained 105 yards on 20 carries, scored on runs of 2 and 7 yards. Fraylon tallied from 15 and 1 yards. Tate, who carried 20 times, scored on a 1-yard plunge.

Central ended its season with a 7-4 record and the Aggies closed out at 3-8.

N.C. Central	14	7	0	14—35
N.C. A&T	0	0	0	7— 7

NCC — Kersey 2 run (Massey kick)
NCC — Fraylon 15 run (Massey kick)
NCC — Fraylon 1 run (Massey kick)
NCC — Tate 1 run (Massey kick)
A&T — Thomas 1 run (Herring kick)
NCC — Kersey 7 run (Massey kick)
Att—14,561 (at Greensboro)

NCCU defeated A&T in Greensboro 35-7 in a game that was never competitive. Head coach Henry "Hank" Lattimore, still smarting from the double losses to the Aggies in 1980, had his charges primed and ready to play. Freshman quarterback Gerald Fraylon scored twice, and the Eagles' Maroon Terror defense held the Aggies to 23 net yards rushing, including multiple quarterback sacks. A&T gifted the Eagles field position and momentum with multiple turnovers. This is a game recap from the *Charlotte Observer* for Sunday, November 29, 1981. (Courtesy of the *Charlotte Observer*.)

In 1982, Maurice "Mo" Forte took over for Jim McKinley as head coach at A&T, and the Aggies defeated NCCU 13-7. A&T's defense was the difference in the 1982 game. A&T came into the game with a 1-7 record, but the defense played with Aggie Pride and refused to lose. They held Benjamin "Ben" Tate to 27 yards on eight carries and sacked Gerald Fraylon eight times. Tate came into the game with 1,009 yards on the season. Meanwhile, A&T's Mike Jones rushed for 113 yards on 26 carries, and Danny Thomas had 105 yards on the ground in 15 attempts. A&T scored first on a 14-yard pass from quarterback Alvin Grier to receiver Jessie Britt. Two field goals followed that. NCCU scored in the fourth quarter on a flea-flicker. NCCU quarterback Gerald Fraylon pitched the ball to Victor Hunter, who tossed a 59-yard strike to Audrain Melton. A&T head coach Merrill Maurice "Mo" Forte played college football for the University of Minnesota, where he starred as a running back from 1966 to 1968. His coaching career began in 1970 at his alma mater. He came to A&T in 1982 from Arizona State, where he coached wide receivers. He coached the Aggies for six seasons. He won a MEAC championship after leading A&T to a 9-3 record and was named MEAC Coach of the Year in 1986. (Courtesy of Atty. Eric Montgomery.)

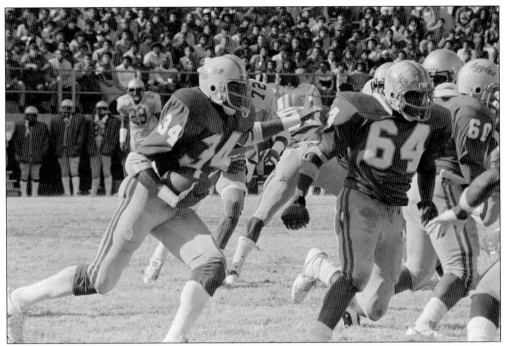

Aggie offensive lineman Harold Ragland (no. 64) pulls to get out in front of running back Mike Jones (no. 34). (Courtesy of the North Carolina Collection Photographic Archives, the Wilson Library, University of North Carolina at Chapel Hill.)

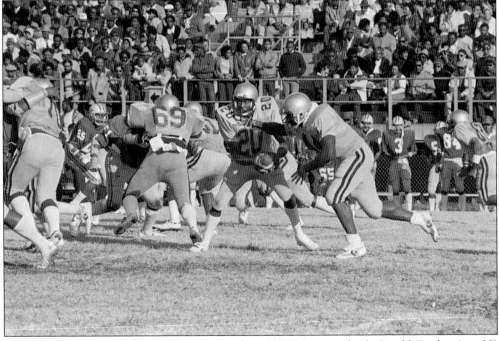

Behind strong blocks by the Eagles offensive line, NCCU quarterback Gerald Fraylon (no. 20) hands off to Benjamin Tate (no. 44). (Courtesy of the North Carolina Collection Photographic Archives, the Wilson Library, University of North Carolina at Chapel Hill.)

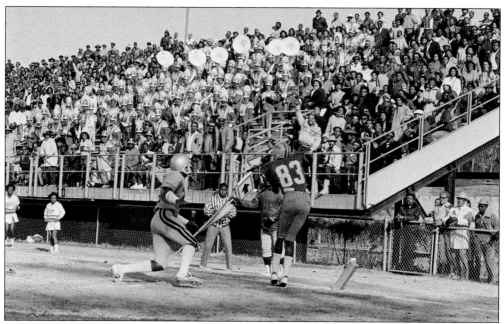

The A&T marching band and Aggie faithful watch from the stands as Jesse Britt (no. 83) catches a touchdown pass in the corner of the end zone. (Courtesy of the North Carolina Collection Photographic Archives, the Wilson Library, University of North Carolina at Chapel Hill.)

Over the long history of the rivalry, the teams have tied five times, including in 1983. Central came into the game favored with a 7-1 record. A&T was 3-6, but Mo Forte's charges started quickly. Aggie quarterback Alvin Grier hit Herbert Harbison for a 25-yard touchdown in the first quarter, and just before the half, Mike Jones scored from one yard out. Mike Jones scored on a short run for NCCU before the half. At the half, the score was A&T 13 and NCCU 7. The Eagles' Maroon Terror defense woke up in the third quarter and shut out the Aggies in the second half. NCCU's Clifton Kersey notched the scores at 13 on a three-yard run in the third quarter. Neither team scored thereafter. NCCU's Reece Carson (no. 33) sheds an Aggies defensive back as A&T linebacker Ricardo Small (no. 55) approaches. (Courtesy of the North Carolina Collection Photographic Archives, the Wilson Library, University of North Carolina at Chapel Hill.)

A swarm of Aggies defensive players has NCCU running back Clifton Kersey (no. 22) surrounded. (Courtesy of the North Carolina Collection Photographic Archives, the Wilson Library, University of North Carolina at Chapel Hill.)

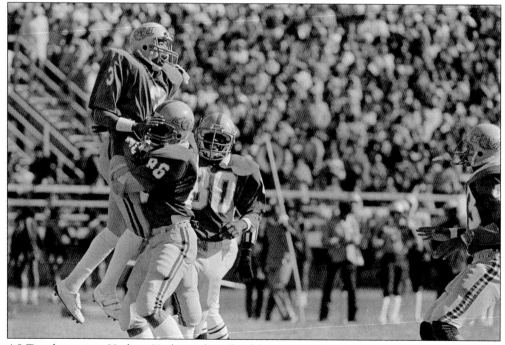

A&T wide receiver Herbert Harbison (no. 3) celebrates a touchdown with teammates. (Courtesy of the North Carolina Collection Photographic Archives, the Wilson Library, University of North Carolina at Chapel Hill.)

NCCU running back Rodney Rivers (no. 26) attempts to split A&T defenders. (Courtesy of the North Carolina Collection Photographic Archives, the Wilson Library, University of North Carolina at Chapel Hill.)

In 1984, the Eagles crushed the Aggies 49-10. At the story's center stood Gerald Fraylon, NCCU's senior quarterback. Fraylon finished his career as NCCU's and the CIAA's all-time leader in passing yards (5,794) and total offense (6,620). Three of his touchdown passes on the day went to Robert Green. Future record-setting wide receiver Robert Clark caught his fourth and final touchdown. NCCU retired Fraylon's jersey after the game. NCCU running back Clifton Kersey added 109 yards on the ground. The Eagles' Maroon Terror defense racked up 11 quarterback sacks. Maynard Smith, James Perry, and Melvin Gaddy each had two. Because of the sacks, A&T had 11 yards rushing on the day. If there was a silver lining for A&T, it was that freshman quarterback Alan Hooker never backed down. He connected with Jesse Britt for a 74-yard touchdown foreshadowing his and A&T's future. Hooker (no. 11) lets a pass fly as NCCU linebacker Marvin Reeves (no. 56) and defensive lineman Melvin Gaddy (no. 93) arrive too late to stop him. Hooker was a running quarterback in high school, but when he finished his career, he was A&T's all-time passing leader. (Courtesy of the North Carolina Collection Photographic Archives, the Wilson Library, University of North Carolina at Chapel Hill.)

Aggies surround NCCU quarterback Gerald Fraylon (no. 20), but on this day, their attempts to stop him were futile. Fraylon threw a rivalry record four touchdowns and 284 yards. Clifton Kersey (no. 22), Eagles running back, is to the right of Fraylon. (Courtesy of the North Carolina Collection Photographic Archives, the Wilson Library, University of North Carolina at Chapel Hill.)

Daryl Webb (no. 26) looks on as Zonta Laney delivers a devastating block to spring Eagles quarterback Gerald Fraylon (no. 20), who looks to pass. (Courtesy of the North Carolina Collection Photographic Archives, the Wilson Library, University of North Carolina at Chapel Hill.)

In 1985, coach Mo Forte and the Aggies avenged the 1984 loss to NCCU by defeating the Eagles 28-19 in Greensboro. A&T quarterback Alan Hooker passed for 237 yards and two touchdowns and sealed the victory with a rushing touchdown. He and A&T wide receiver Jesse Britt were named MEAC Players of the Week. Britt had six receptions for 109 yards. NCCU quarterback Earl "Air" Harvey set a rivalry record by passing for 360 yards. Robert Clark accounted for 180 of those yards. Hooker marched the Aggies on a 70-yard touchdown drive to open the game. He connected with Juan Jackson for a nine-yard touchdown. Harvey answered for NCCU on its opening possession. He led the Eagles on a 72-yard scoring drive that ended on an eight-yard touchdown pass to Robert Green. Central went ahead of A&T on its next possession when Leon Humphrey scored from two yards out. In the second quarter, Hooker drove the Aggies 89 yards on 12 plays. His four-yard touchdown pass to Herb Harbison put A&T up 14-13. Again, Harvey answered, guiding the Eagles on a 61-yard scoring drive. Harvey ran the final four yards for the score on a bootleg. NCCU led at the half 19-14. It rained during the second half, and A&T's defense increased in intensity. It sacked NCCU's freshman phenom eight times and shut down the Eagles' rushing attack. In the third quarter, A&T went on top 21-19 after fullback Stoney Polite scored on a 14-yard run. Later in the quarter, Hooker scored on a short run. Herb Harbison hauls in one of his four receptions. He finished the day with 73 yards receiving. (Courtesy of North Carolina A&T State University Archives and Special Collections.)

As the football team took it to the Eagles, A&T's band kept the Aggies rocking in the stands. (Courtesy of North Carolina A&T State University Archives and Special Collections.)

NCCU's record-setting quarterback James Earl "Air" Harvey is pictured as a freshman. "Air" Harvey set 81 school records at NCCU and 15 Division II passing records. In 1985, he became the first freshman in NCAA history to pass for more than 3,000 yards. He was an American Football Coaches Association first-team All-American in 1988, not bad for a quarterback who infrequently threw in high school. (Courtesy of the North Carolina Collection Photographic Archives, the Wilson Library, University of North Carolina at Chapel Hill.)

N.C. A&T 28, NCCU 19

N.C. Central	13 6 0 0	—19
N.C. A&T	7 7 14 0	—28

A&T—Jackson 9 pass from Hooker (Levett kick)
NCCU—Green 8 pass from Harvey (Huey kick)
NCCU—Humphrey 2 run (kick failed)
A&T—Harbison 4 pass from Hooker (Levett kick)
NCCU—Harvey 4 run (pass failed)
A&T—Polite 14 run (Levett kick)
A&T—Hooker 3 run (Levett kick)
A—10,500.

	NCCU	A&T
First downs	19	26
Rushes-yards	24-(-49)	42-272
Passing yards	360	237
Passes	21-38-1	16-25-1
Punts	3-34	2-31
Fumbles-lost	4-2	5-3
Penalties-yards	7- 65	11-98
Time of possession	22:43	37:17

INDIVIDUAL

RUSHING—NCCU: Humphrey 3-3, Rivers 3-2, Oakley 1-0, Webb 1-0, Harvey 15-(minus 45). **A&T:** Polite 29-203, Shivers 8-51, Jackson 2-7, Hooker 12-(minus 3), Gee 2-26.

PASSING—NCCU: Harvey 21-38-1-360. **A&T:** Hooker 16-25-1-237.

RECEIVING—NCCU: Clark 9-180, Oakley 5-88, Green 3-40, Rivers 224, McNeil 2-20. **A&T:** Britt 6-107, Harbison 4-73, Polite 2-25, Best 1-13, Jackson 1-9, Johnson 1-5, Shivers 1-5.

A box score from the *Durham Morning Herald* for Sunday, November 17, 1985, shows the impressive statistics of Earl "Air" Harvey, Alan Hooker, Stoney Polite, and Robert Clark. (Courtesy of the *Durham Morning Herald*.)

In 1986, A&T came to Durham with an 8-1 record, defeated NCCU 35-12, and captured the MEAC title. Hooker played a sensational game. He threw for 185 yards and rushed for 76. A&T forced seven turnovers, including four interceptions of Harvey. Aggies defensive back Joe Summersett picked off three. Harvey passed for 242 yards. Senior Eagles receivers Robert Clark and Robert Green each caught multiple receptions and completed their careers having caught a pass in every game they played at NCCU. Freshman fullback Gary Leath scored on a 12-yard run to give NCCU the early lead, but A&T scored the next five touchdowns. Hooker scored on two long runs in the first quarter and passed to Anthony Best for a six-yard touchdown in the second. A&T led 21-6 at the half. In the third, Aggies fullback Stoney Polite scored on a one-yard plunge, and Joe Summersett returned an interception 67 yards for a touchdown. On the final play, Green caught a four-yard touchdown pass from Harvey. Central finished the season 6-4. Alan Hooker looks to pass during the 1985 victory over the Eagles in Durham. In 1986, Hooker was MEAC Offensive Player of the Year and Black College Football Player of the Year. (Courtesy of the *Durham Morning Herald*.)

Robert Clark played his final season for NCCU in 1986. A Richmond, Virginia, native, Clark finished his career at NCCU as a four-time All-Conference selection and the all-time receiver in CIAA history with 210 receptions for 4,231 yards and 38 touchdowns. NCCU retired his jersey after the game. (Courtesy of the *Durham Morning Herald*.)

Durham Morning Herald/**Charles Ledford**

Eagle cheerleaders for 1986 show off their balance and athleticism. (Courtesy of North Carolina Central University Archives–James E. Shepard Memorial Library.)

NCCU 38, N.C. A&T 19

N.C. Central	7	14	10	7—38
N.C. A&T	6	0	6	7—19

NCC—Hargrove 15 pass from Harvey (Stinson kick)

A&T—Polite 7 run (kick failed)

NCC—McNeil 7 pass from Harvey (Stinson kick)

NCC—Leath 2 pass from Harvey (Stinson kick)

NCC—FG Stinson 43

A&T—Jackson 1 run (kick blocked)

NCC—Burt 16 run (Stinson kick)

A&T—Best 6 pass from Hooker (Gotson kick)

NCC—Leath 7 pass Harvey (Stinson kick)

A—20,000.

	NCC	A&T
First downs	24	25
Rushes-yards	53-187	30-149
Passing	333	324
Return Yards	6	0
Comp-Att-Int	22-37-0	26-42-3
Punts	2-40	4-40
Fumbles-Lost	3-3	5-3
Penalties-Yards	7-56	18-178

INDIVIDUAL STATISTICS

Rushing—N.C. Central, Harvey 14-72, Burt 13-78, Oakley 9-34, Leath 4-2, Wiggins 1-(-5), Best 2-7. N.C. A&T, Polite 11-66, Hooker 9-34, Jackson 7-8, McLean 3-41.

Passing—N.C. Central, Harvey 22-37-0-333, Best 1-1-0-12, Oakley 0-1-0-0. N.C. A&T, Hooker 26-42-3-324.

Receiving—N.C. Central, Leath 8-117, Hargrove 4-84, McNeill 4-44, Vanhook 4-60, Oakley 2-28. N.C. A&T, Best 9-148, Sowell 8-106, Johnson 4-51, Polite 3-2, Jackson 2-17.

In 1987, NCCU defeated A&T 38-19 in Greensboro. Junior Eagle quarterback Earl "Air" Harvey passed for 321 yards and four touchdowns (a game high) and rushed for 72 yards. Aggie quarterback Alan Hooker spent the day running for his life but still passed for 324 yards and a touchdown. The Eagles picked him off three times and recovered three A&T fumbles. In 1987, as seen in this *Durham Morning Herald* box score, Earl "Air" Harvey and Alan Hooker each passed for over 300 yards. (Courtesy of the *Durham Morning Herald*.)

In 1988, the regular-season game between the Aggies and Eagles was played during a month other than November for the first time since 1948. On September 3 under the lights at O'Kelly-Riddick field, NCCU defeated A&T 15-2. Hank Lattimore and the Eagles owned this day. NCCU's touchdowns came on David Burt's five-yard run and Anthony Cooley's 33-yard touchdown reception from senior quarterback Earl "Air" Harvey. A&T's only points came on an errand snap that went over the head of Harvey and out of the back of the end zone for an Aggies safety. In 1988, A&T hired Bill Hayes from Winston-Salem State. Hayes was the next in a line of great Aggie coaches that extends back to Lonnie Pfunander Byarm, who won A&T's first CIAA title in 1927. No coach before or after Hayes accomplished what he did in the rivalry. A Durham native and proud Hillside High School alumnus, Hayes is also a former All-American center and linebacker for his beloved coach Herman Riddick and an alumnus of NCC. He holds the record for most coached victories (12) and most consecutive victories (12) in the rivalry. Hayes won three MEAC championships and two HBCU national titles and is A&T's all-time winningest coach. (Courtesy of Atty. Eric Montgomery.)

Earl "Air" Harvey (no. 10), the NCCU quarterback, looks to pass. Harvey once considered not going to college but instead staying home in Fayetteville and bagging groceries. It's a good thing for NCCU that he decided to be an Eagle. In 1988, "His Airness" passed for a remarkable 2,369 yards and 22 touchdowns. (Courtesy of the North Carolina Collection Photographic Archives, the Wilson Library, University of North Carolina at Chapel Hill.)

Several Aggie defensive players sack Eagles quarterback Earl "Air" Harvey. (Courtesy of the North Carolina Collection Photographic Archives, the Wilson Library, University of North Carolina at Chapel Hill.)

A&T quarterback Hilton Winstead (no. 19) evades Eagle defender David Coleman II (no. 55). (Courtesy of the North Carolina Collection Photographic Archives, the Wilson Library, University of North Carolina at Chapel Hill.)

Harvey keeps his eyes downfield and the ball in the cocked and ready-to-launch position while running away from an Aggies defensive player. (Courtesy of the North Carolina Collection Photographic Archives, the Wilson Library, University of North Carolina at Chapel Hill.)

openers.

N.C. Central 15, N.C. A&T 2:
Earl Harvey became the all-time total offensive leader in NCAA Division II history, passing for 176 yards and one touchdown to lead North Carolina Central over North Carolina A&T.

Harvey had games with better statistics, but he did enough against A&T to vault him to the top of Division II football total offensive leaders. (Courtesy of the *Greenville Sun*.)

Aggies Thump Eagles, 24-6

By ED PRICE
Herald sports writer

Connell Maynor threw for 288 yards and three touchdowns in A&T's 24-6 win over the Eagles in 1989. A sophomore transfer quarterback from Winston-Salem State University, Maynor had a coming-out party in the A&T victory at Aggie Stadium. Nearly 18,000 spectators were in attendance. NCCU opened the scoring in the first quarter with a 53-yard touchdown drive, but those were all the points Aggies All-American linebacker Demetrius Harrison and the A&T defense allowed. Eagles quarterback Rick Witcher had a long day against A&T, but he got the Maroon and Gray on the scoreboard first with an 18-yard touchdown pass to tight end Anthony Cooley. From then on, it was all A&T. Maynor completed touchdown passes to Freddy Brown, Jeff Watson, and Jerome Crawford. Billy Wehunt also contributed a field goal for A&T. (Courtesy of the *Durham Morning Herald*.)

116

This is the *Rocky Mount Telegram* newspaper's summary for the 1989 game. (Courtesy of the *Rocky Mount Telegram*.)

In this photograph from the *A&T Register*, Connell Maynor (no. 2) passes the ball during the 1989 game. Maynor followed Coach Hayes to A&T from Winston-Salem State. In 1990 and 1991, Maynor was MEAC Offensive Player of the Year. In 1990, he led the Aggies to their third Black College Championship. (Courtesy of North Carolina A&T State University Archives and Special Collections.)

Maynor drives Aggies to victory over Eagles

N.C. A&T 21
N.C. Central 6

CHARLOTTE — Russell Manor threw two fourth-quarter touchdown passes as North Carolina A&T defeated North Carolina Central in a season-opening game Saturday.

The Aggies held a 7-6 lead heading into the final quarter, but struck for two quick touchdowns to seal the victory.

Tommy McCoy's 16-yard interception with 14:15 left helped set up Manor's 6-yard scoring strike to Russell McClain a minute later.

Manor then put the contest out of reach when he hit Jim Mar Leizey with an 8-yard TD pass midway through the final period.

N. Carolina A&T	7	0	0	14—21
N.C. Central	0	6	0	0—6

A&T—C. Maynor 8 run (V. Maynor kick)
NCC—Gary 3 run (kick failed)
A&T—McClain 6 pass from C. Maynor (V. Maynor kick)
A&T—Leitzey 8 pass from Maynor (V. Maynor kick)
A—14,800.

	A&T	NCC
First downs	14	11
Rushes-yards	39-168	30-72
Passing	174	111
Return Yards	120	39
Comp-Att-Int	12-19-2	17-39-2
Punts	8-35	10-37
Fumbles-Lost	2-1	1-1
Penalties-Yards	7-70	4-40
Time of Possession	31:30	28:30

INDIVIDUAL STATISTICS

RUSHING—N. Carolina A&T, Turner 4-46, McClain 5-28, C. Maynor 9-22. N.C. Central, B. Harris 9-26, Gary 5-19.

PASSING—N. Carolina A&T, C. Maynor 12-18-1-111, Parker 1-0-1-0. N.C. Central, Brewington 17-39-2-174.

RECEIVING—N. Carolina A&T, Prince 1-31, Cooper 2-28, L. Jackson 2-25. N.C. Central, Cooley 5-63, Hargrove 3-44, Hill 4-37.

A&T scored two touchdowns in the fourth quarter in 1990 to put away a closely contested game. Connell Maynor ran for one score and threw touchdowns to Tommy McCoy and Jarmal Leitzey. The Aggies defense held the Eagles to six points for the second year. The game was played in Charlotte. In 1990, coach Bill Hayes and quarterback Connell Maynor led A&T to a 9-2 record and an HBCU championship. After the season, Maynor was named MEAC Offensive Player of the Year. He led NCAA I-AA quarterbacks in passing efficiency. The game headline from the *Durham Morning Herald* for Sunday, September 2, 1990, highlights the outstanding play of Maynor. (Courtesy of the *Durham Morning Herald*.)

Here is the *Greenville News* game summary for the 1990 contest played in Charlotte, North Carolina. (Courtesy of the *Greenville News*.)

In 1991, the Aggies ran around and over NCCU 48-0, the largest margin in series history to that date. In 1964, Bert Piggott walloped NCCU 46-0, but Bill Hayes's victory in 1991 was a harbinger for the rest of the decade. Moreover, Hayes baptized NCCU's first-year head coach Bishop Harris by fire. The Aggies rushed for a remarkable 441 yards using 13 different ball carriers while holding NCCU to net four yards rushing. A&T's defense sacked NCCU's quarterbacks 10 times. With the victory, Coach Hayes won his first and A&T its third MEAC championship. During the 1991 game, NCCU linebacker George Harden (no. 56) tackles A&T running back Barry Turner (no. 21). (Courtesy of the North Carolina Collection Photographic Archives, the Wilson Library, University of North Carolina at Chapel Hill.)

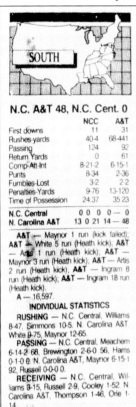

A box score for the 1991 game from the *Orlando Sentinel* reveals just how dominant A&T was. (Courtesy of the *Orlando Sentinel*.)

Barry Turner carried A&T to a 49-7 victory at O'Kelly-Riddick Stadium in 1992, and A&T won the MEAC championship, its fourth and coach Bill Hayes's second. Turner rushed for 100 yards for the Aggies, who piled up an ungodly 519 yards total offense to NCCU's 95. In the first quarter, NCCU scored first on tailback Joe Simmon's four-yard run around the left end. After that, it was all A&T. The Aggies followed a Carl Warren field goal with seven unanswered touchdowns by Barry Turner, James Lancaster, Brian Rodman, Adrian Starks, Fred Ingram, Michael Artis, and Sherwood Jones. A few failed extra points made the Aggies' final score 49 rather than 52. Future star quarterbacks Maseo Bolin for A&T and Brad McAdams for NCCU played in the rivalry for the first time. Richard Lide (no. 63), Aggies center, leads the right side of the offensive line in blocking for running back Mike Artis, who takes a handoff from quarterback David Russell (no. 17). An Eagles linebacker (no. 58) prepares to make the tackle on Artis. (Courtesy of the North Carolina Collection Photographic Archives, the Wilson Library, University of North Carolina at Chapel Hill.)

Bishop Harris points instructions while Eagle players huddle on the sideline. Harris was the second African American assistant football coach in the Atlantic Coast Conference (ACC). He began his collegiate coaching career as a graduate assistant at Duke University in 1972. Bill Hayes, then head coach of A&T and Harris's opponent that day, was the first African American assistant football coach in the ACC. He began his collegiate coaching career at Wake Forest University. Both Hayes and Harris are NCCU alumni. (Courtesy of the North Carolina Collection Photographic Archives, the Wilson Library, University of North Carolina at Chapel Hill.)

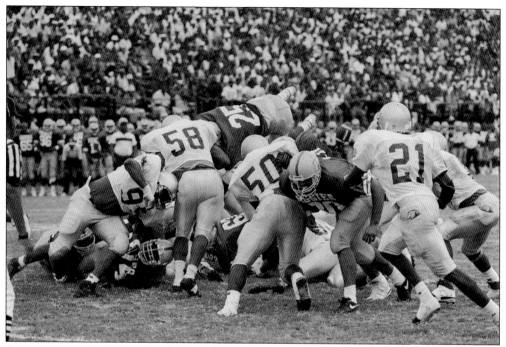

A capacity crowd at NCCU's O'Kelly-Riddick Stadium watches A&T running back Gilbert Jones (no. 25) fumble while attempting to dive over a gang of Aggies blockers and Eagles defenders for a first down. (Courtesy of the North Carolina Collection Photographic Archives, the Wilson Library, University of North Carolina at Chapel Hill.)

Eagles dancing girls watch A&T running back Barry Turner (no. 21) carry the ball like a loaf of bread and turn the corner on the Eagles defense. Beloved NCCU alumnus and photographer Robert Lawson (right) can be seen holding his camera. (Courtesy of the North Carolina Collection Photographic Archives, the Wilson Library, University of North Carolina at Chapel Hill.)

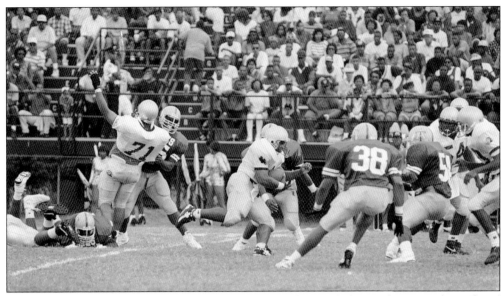

Joe Simmons (no. 3) weaves his way through Aggie defenders, including Robert Gray (no. 38) and Delaney McKinnon (no. 54). Simmons went on to become NCCU's all-time leading rusher. Greg Pruitt Jr. later passed him. (Courtesy of the North Carolina Collection Photographic Archives, the Wilson Library, University of North Carolina at Chapel Hill.)

The teams did not play in 1993. In 1994, the Eagles and Aggies played in the inaugural Aggie-Eagle Classic. Played in Raleigh, North Carolina, at Carter-Finley Stadium, A&T soundly defeated NCCU 38-9. For A&T, David Perry rushed for two TDs, Maseo Bolin threw for a TD, and the Aggies scored two TDs off turnovers. NCCU quarterback Brad McAdams passed for 108 yards but was intercepted twice. NCCU turned the ball over seven times. Their lone touchdown came on an 11-yard pass from senior quarterback Corey Redfern. The final score was 38-9 Aggies. This was NCCU Head Coach Larry Little's first game against the Aggies. Little played college football at Bethune Cookman and was an All-Pro Guard for the Miami Dolphins in the 1970s. He replaced Bishop Harris at Central and was inducted into the Pro Football Hall of Fame in 1993. A receiver checks with the Aggies sideline before the ball snap. (Courtesy of Atty. Eric Montgomery.)

As the Eagles' expressions clearly convey, the Aggies did not give them much to cheer for. (Courtesy of DigitalNC.org Yearbook Online Archive.)

The 1995 game was the closest since 1983, when the teams played to a 13-13 tie. Over 44,000 fans watched A&T pull out a come-from-behind victory over the Eagles by the slimmest of margins, 18-17. NCCU raced out to a 17-0 first-half lead behind the play of senior quarterback Brad McAdams, who was 9-14 for 135 yards in the half. Billy Massey and Todd McGuire scored rushing touchdowns for the Eagles, but NCCU missed two field goals that would have extended the lead. McAdams had blurred vision at the half, so coach Larry Little put Duran McLaurin in for the third quarter. That's when the Aggies made their move. A&T quarterback Maseo Bolin and James Bowden lead the comeback with assistance from a rejuvenated defense. Bolin connected with Bowden on a 64-yard score in the third quarter and a 49-yard score early in the fourth. McAdams returned to the game, but A&T had seized the momentum by then. Milton Shaw scored the game-winning touchdown for the Aggies in the fourth quarter. NCCU defensive lineman Dawson Odoms (no. 55), with fire in his eyes, hotly pursues Milton Shaw (no. 20), A&T running back. In 2012, Southern University in Baton Rouge, Louisiana, appointed Odoms head coach. From 2012 to 2020, Odoms went 53-16 in the SWAC. In 2021, Odoms took over the head coaching job at Norfolk State University. (Courtesy of the North Carolina Collection Photographic Archives, the Wilson Library, University of North Carolina at Chapel Hill.)

Eagles quarterback Brad McAdams (no. 16) looks to make a short pass. McAdams is fifth amongst Eagles career passing leaders with 5,687 yards. (Courtesy of the North Carolina Collection Photographic Archives, the Wilson Library, University of North Carolina at Chapel Hill.)

Eagles defenders gang tackle Aggie running back Milton Shaw (no. 20). (Courtesy of the North Carolina Collection Photographic Archives, the Wilson Library, University of North Carolina at Chapel Hill.)

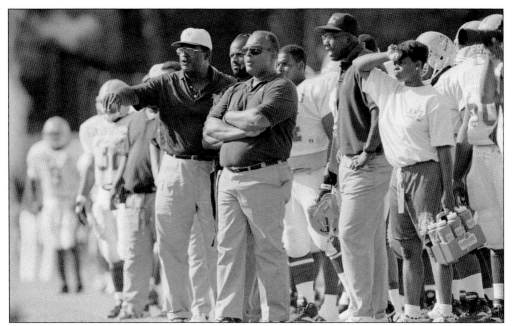

Looking on from the A&T sideline, from left to right, are senior quarterback Maseo Bolin (no. 9), Lafaunte Smith (no. 32), coach Mark Sanders (obscured), coach Bill Wehunt (obscured), head coach Bill Hayes, coach Jack Cameron (headset), coach Robert Pulliam (arms crossed), Charles Alexander (94), coach Eric Carr, Ieshia Graham-Allen, and Chad Mann (60). (Courtesy of the North Carolina Collection Photographic Archives, The Wilson Library, University of North Carolina at Chapel Hill.)

Maseo Bolin (no. 9), quarterback, keeps his eyes downfield while he attempts to break free from the clutches of an Eagle defender (no. 32). A four-year starter, Bolin set the A&T single-season passing record with 2,262 yards in 1995 and is the Aggies' third all-time leading passer, with 6,607 yards. (Courtesy of the North Carolina Collection Photographic Archives, the Wilson Library, University of North Carolina at Chapel Hill.)

Buddy Crutchfield helped anchor the best defensive backfield in Division II football. Here he gets the facemask of A&T's Milton Shaw. Crutchfield played professionally for the Washington Redskins and New York Jets. (Courtesy of the *Durham Morning Herald*.)

A&T outdueled NCCU in overtime in 1996. The Aggies jumped to a 28-7 lead before Brad McAdams came to life and threw five touchdowns. Three of those went to Antione Calloway. Leading by three points, NCCU thought the game was sealed in regulation when Eagles safety Trei Oliver picked off Ben Garrett's pass late in the fourth quarter, but game officials called roughing the passer against NCCU, and A&T got 15 yards and a fresh set of downs. Luther Leak kicked a 27-yard field goal with two seconds left in regulation to tie the game. Michael Basnight scored from the NCCU seven-yard line in overtime to give A&T a 38-31 victory over the Eagles. NCCU head coach Larry Little exhorts his charges during the game in 1996. Little was an All-Pro guard on the 1972 Super Bowl champion Miami Dolphins team that went undefeated. An alumnus of Bethune-Cookman College, where he starred as a football player, Little was head coach at his alma mater from 1983 to 1991. He was head coach at NCCU from 1993 to 1998. His best team was the 1996 Eagles, which went 8-3 and finished fourth in the CIAA. (Courtesy of the North Carolina Collection Photographic Archives, the Wilson Library, University of North Carolina at Chapel Hill.)

NCCU senior quarterback Brad McAdams threw for 309 yards and five touchdowns in the 38-31 overtime loss to the Aggies. A&T defensemen Toran James (no. 57) and Wayne Shuford (no. 40) attempt to get McAdams down before he can pass the ball. (Courtesy of the North Carolina Collection Photographic Archives, the Wilson Library, University of North Carolina at Chapel Hill.)

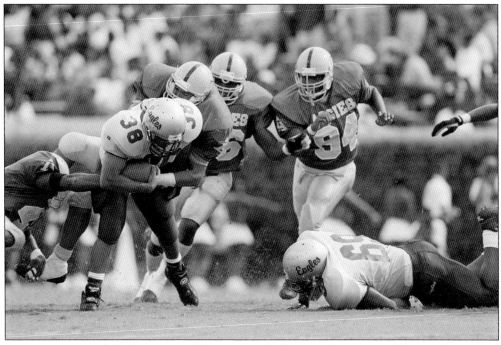

A swarm of Aggie defenders gang tackles an Eagle ball carrier. (Courtesy of the North Carolina Collection Photographic Archives, the Wilson Library, University of North Carolina at Chapel Hill.)

Michael Basnight (no. 35) scores the game-winning touchdown in overtime to knock off NCCU 38-31. Theron Thomas III (ball boy, center) is in the background holding the ball with both hands. He played cornerback at NCA&T from 2002 to 2005; his father was equipment manager at NCA&T from 1984 to 2019. (Courtesy of the North Carolina Collection Photographic Archives, the Wilson Library, University of North Carolina at Chapel Hill.)

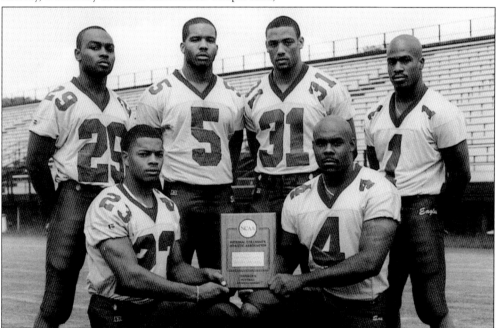

NCCU's record-setting defensive backfield in 1996, Michael Wall (no. 29), Chris Thompson (no. 23), Buddy Crutchfield (no. 5), Trei Oliver (no. 31), Travis Sadler (no. 4), and Adrian Jones (no. 1), led all NCAA Division II teams in pass defense. Jones is the head coach at Shaw University. Oliver is the current head coach at NCCU and intercepted a pass in the 1996 Aggie-Eagle Classic. (Courtesy of the North Carolina Collection Photographic Archives, the Wilson Library, University of North Carolina at Chapel Hill.)

In 1997, A&T started fast. Running back Michael Basnight scored two first-quarter touchdowns. The second came after NCCU quarterback Warren Bell fumbled, and A&T linebacker Shawn Paylor recovered the ball. In the second quarter, Aggies quarterback Ben Garrett, who completed 15 passes for 168 yards, connected with receiver Henry Douglas for a 25-yard touchdown. The lone bright spot for the Eagles was an 11-play, 80-yard drive that led to a short touchdown pass from Bell to Jelani Manuel just before the half. It was 20-7 A&T at the break. Ben Garret scored on a one-yard quarterback keeper in the middle of the third quarter. Matt Baldwin gave A&T a 29-7 lead at the end of the third quarter. With less than three minutes remaining, James Bullock scored a touchdown on a short run. The final score was A&T 36 and NCCU 7. Coach Bill Hayes was asked probing questions about why his team threw the ball late in the fourth quarter ahead by three touchdowns. NCCU's coach Larry Little and many Eagles felt Hayes was running the score up. Hayes was unfazed and indicated that A&T had to prepare for the rest of its season. Jay Reid (no. 52) and his Aggie teammates are pictured as they celebrate an A&T touchdown. (Courtesy of the *Durham Morning Herald*.)

This box score for the game appeared in the *Rocky Mount Telegram* on Sunday, August 31, 1997. (Courtesy of the *Rocky Mount Telegram*.)

N.C. A&T 36,
N.C. Central 7

N.C. A&T	14	6	9	7—36
N.C. Central	0	7	0	0— 7

First Quarter
NCA&T—Basnight 16 run (Baldwin kick), 5:32
NCA&T—Basnight 14 run (Baldwin kick), 1:24
Second Quarter
NCA&T—Douglas 25 pass from Garrett (kick failed), 9:10
NCCU—Manuel 3 pass from Bell (Masih kick), 00:56
Third Quarter
NCA&T—Garrett 1 run (kick failed), 8:32
NCA&T—FG Baldwin 27, 00:38
Fourth Quarter
NCA&T—Bullock 1 run (Baldwin kick), 2:31
A—48,001.

INDIVIDUAL STATISTICS
RUSHING—N.C. A&T, Basnight 12-76, Shuford 11-59, Smith 7-48, Garrett 13-26, Wallace 1-2, Bullock 1-1, Stone 3-(-1), Woodruff 1-(-7). N.C. Central, Gibbs 12-35, Bulla 3-3, Flowers 4-2, McGuire 3-(-1), Bell 11-(-23).
PASSING—N.C. A&T, Garrett 7-15-0-168, Woodruff 2-2-0-11. N.C. Central, Bell 15-28-2-153.
RECEIVING—N.C. A&T, Douglas 3-77, Smith 2-39, Pelshak 1-22, Basnight 1-22, Shuford 1-13, White 1-7. N.C. Central, Gibbs 5-46, McCathern 2-30, Manuel 2-28, Hammond 2-15, Brown 2-14, Brodie 1-16, McGuire 1-4.

In 1998, A&T defeated NCCU 40-10 for what was Coach Bill Hayes's ninth consecutive victory over the Eagles. No coach in the then 76-year-old series won more games than Bill Hayes. NCCU fans must understand that Hayes's love for NCCU was not diminished by his success as A&T's coach against his alma mater. For Hayes, it was simple: he had gone into the homes and hearts of the young men who played for him at A&T, and he committed to their success for a lifetime, even against NCCU. That NCCU was a Division II school mattered little to Hayes. That had nothing to do with A&T. The Eagles are the Aggies' biggest rival, and the game was an opportunity for his players to win and get better. Hayes made the most of that opportunity, more than any other coach before or after. In sum, Hayes did exactly what A&T paid him to do as head coach, and his success was not limited to defeating NCCU. No A&T head football coach has won as many games (106) as Bill Hayes before or since. (Courtesy of the North Carolina Collection Photographic Archives, the Wilson Library, University of North Carolina at Chapel Hill.)

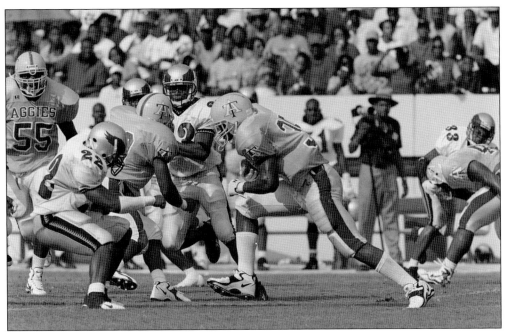

Michael Basnight (no. 35) cuts upfield as NCCU defenders, including Chris Thompson (no. 23) and Michael Royals (no. 33), track the ball carrier. Omnipresent NCCU alumnus and photographer Robert Lawson is in the background holding a camera. (Courtesy of the North Carolina Collection Photographic Archives, the Wilson Library, University of North Carolina at Chapel Hill.)

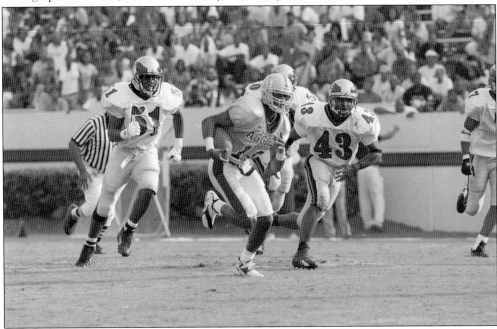

Aggies wide receiver Marcus Ragsdale (no. 10), son of A&T football great George Ragsdale, has an open field in front of him and turns on the jets. Jamar Green (no. 43), Maurice Blanding (no. 7), Anthony Connaly (no. 50), and other Eagles give chase. (Courtesy of the North Carolina Collection Photographic Archives, the Wilson Library, University of North Carolina at Chapel Hill.)

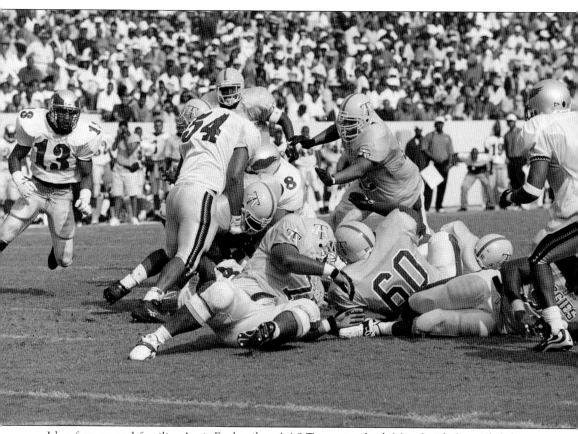

It's a famous and familiar Aggie-Eagle pile-up! A&T running back Moe Smith (no. 43) fights to get into the end zone and gets help from the Aggies offensive line: Carroll "Roc" Burley (no. 62), Greg Coley (no. 79), Adrian Thompkins (no. 75), Chad Mann (no. 60), and Bryant Hernandez (no. 51). Weak-side linebacker Mike Harris (no. 54) leads teammates Cory Francis (no. 98), defensive tackle; Kevin Peoples (no. 13), strong-side linebacker; and Maurice Blanding (no. 7), free safety, in stopping Smith. (Courtesy of the North Carolina Collection Photographic Archives, the Wilson Library, University of North Carolina at Chapel Hill.)

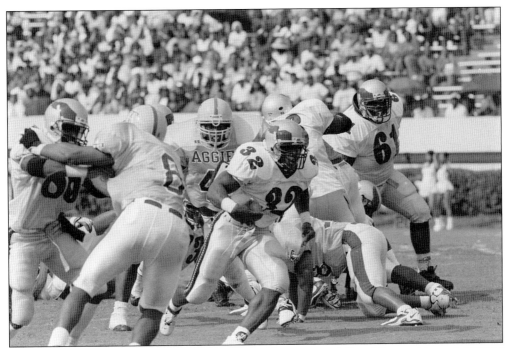

With the help of teammates Reggie Mideau (no. 61), center, and David Pratt, tight end, NCCU fullback Junior Bulla (no. 32) knifes through the A&T defense. (Courtesy of the North Carolina Collection Photographic Archives, the Wilson Library, University of North Carolina at Chapel Hill.)

A&T's high-stepping Blue & Gold Marching Machine show off their moves. (Courtesy of Atty. Eric Montgomery.)

NCCU's enchanting dancing girls leave the stands to perform for halftime. (Courtesy of Atty. Eric Montgomery.)

In 1999, A&T defeated NCCU and won an MEAC and an HBCU championship. It rained the entire game, and neither team played their best football, but A&T did enough to win. The Aggies' defense was relentless the entire game and pitched a shutout for the first three quarters. After the game, new NCCU head coach Rudy Abrams contributed A&T's advantage to their 2-1 football scholarship ratio over NCCU and bigger offensive and defensive linemen. A&T head coach Bill Hayes refused to apologize for his talent advantage. A&T opened with a five-play, 74-yard scoring drive that took 1 minute and 42 seconds. The key plays were Romando North's 44-yard run to the Eagles' 17-yard line and Eric Farmer's 17-yard touchdown run. Farmer added a second first-quarter touchdown run a few minutes later. That put A&T up 14-0. Daren Dawkins added a couple of field goals for the Aggies. NCCU quarterback Durant McCathern prevented the shutout by leading an 11-play, 65-yard drive in the fourth quarter. His 12-yard touchdown pass to Mike Hill was the Eagles' only score. (Courtesy of the *Durham Morning Herald*.)

A&T defensive tackle Leonard Reliford (no. 92) celebrates sacking Durant McCathern (no. 9). (Courtesy of the *Durham Morning Herald*.)

In 1999, NCCU hired Thomas "Rudy" Abrams away from Livingstone College in Salisbury, North Carolina, where he had been head coach since 1994. Abrams was head coach at NCCU from 1999 to 2002. In 2002, his team broke A&T's 12-game winning streak against NCCU. (Courtesy of the North Carolina Collection Photographic Archives, the Wilson Library, University of North Carolina at Chapel Hill.)

Five

A New Millennium for an Old Rivalry
2000–Present

The new millennium ushered in an era of changes and excitement for the rivalry as both programs achieved unparalleled success on the gridiron. The long-running Aggie-Eagle Classic, played each year at Carter-Finley Stadium in Raleigh since 1994, switched back to the respective campuses of the two schools. Also important to the series, NCCU returned to the MEAC in 2010, moving from NCAA Division II to Division I. This significantly increased the number of scholarships available for the football team. As a Division II program, NCCU had less than half the number of scholarship football players as A&T.

Coach Bill Hayes started the Aggies off in the new millennium with back-to-back wins against NCCU, which increased his series record to 12-1. Wide receiver Ramondo North, cornerback Curtis Deloatch, and running back Maurice Hicks were difference makers for the Aggies in those games, and all three later played in the NFL. In 2002, the biggest comeback in series history occurred when the Eagles came from 27 points down to win in overtime and break Hayes's victory streak. Running back Donnie Pippen's leaping score won the game for NCCU. Quarterback Lawrence Fuller, wide receiver Nathaniel Fitch, and defensive back Hassan Smith came up big for NCCU head coach Rudy Abrams that game.

In 2003, A&T hired George Small, a former Aggies player. Small and the Aggies rode running back Frank Patterson and the game-altering defense of linebacker Joey Lance over the Eagles to start the season and went on to win the MEAC title. Small was named MEAC Coach of the Year. He went 2-1 against the Eagles. In 2003, Rod Broadway got his first head coaching job at NCCU, where he coached for four years. In 2005, NCC defeated A&T and won the CIAA and a national title. In 2006, the Eagles had two All-American offensive linemen, Sam Funches and Robert Duncan. The team completed the regular season undefeated and won the CIAA and their third national championship. Broadway went 29-5 from 2004 to 2006 at NCCU. Defensive back Craig Amos, receiver Brandon Alston, defensive back Andre George, linebacker Naim Abdul-Malik, and quarterback Stadford Brown starred for the Eagles. In 2007, Mose Rison became head coach and went 3-1 against A&T.

In 2011, Broadway became head coach at A&T. Over the next seven seasons, A&T went 4-3 versus NCCU, shared conference titles in 2014 and 2015, won an outright title in 2017, and won national championships in 2015 and 2017. Running back Tarik Cohen and quarterback Lamar Raynard starred for A&T and played in the NFL. Broadway stepped down at the end of the 2017 season. In 2018, Sam Washington replaced Broadway and won MEAC championships and national titles in 2018 and 2019. Washington had previously been the defensive coordinator on Larry Little's staff at NCCU (1993–2000). Following the dismissal of Washington in December 2022, in January 2023 Vincent Brown was introduced as A&T's head coach.

When NCCU hired Jerry Mack in 2014 at 34 years old, he was one of the youngest head coaches in Division I college football. Mack's Eagles won three straight against A&T (2014–2016) and a share of the MEAC title in 2014 and 2015. They were alone at the top of the conference in 2016 and participated in the Celebration Bowl in Atlanta, Georgia. Much of the team's success can be attributed to the outstanding quarterback play of Malcolm Bell, who set single-season total offense records in 2014, 2015, and 2016.

After almost 100 years of competition, the rivalry remains strong, and interest in the game remains high. But the rivalry is far more than just a game. It embodies the pride, commitment, spirit of excellence, and determination that set both institutions apart from their peers and define what it truly means to be an Eagle or an Aggie.

Lightning delayed the game by an hour and 48 minutes in 2000. Once the game started, turnovers turned out to be the difference. In the third quarter, A&T led NCCU 14-7. The Eagles had the ball and a chance to score but fumbled two yards short of the goal line. A&T linebacker Sammie Rogers recovered the fumble and raced 98 yards for an Aggies touchdown and a 20-7 lead. The game got away from NCCU from that point, as A&T scored the next 20 points to make the final score 40-7. The victory was A&T's 11th in a row. A *Durham Morning Herald* photograph shows Durant McCathern, a senior wide receiver for NCCU from Greensboro, North Carolina. McCathern was offensive MVP for the game in 1998 as a wide receiver. In 1999, he played quarterback. He was switched back to wide receiver for his final game against the Aggies in 2000. (Courtesy of the *Durham Morning Herald*.)

By the turn of the millennium, A&T had rolled off 11 consecutive victories. NCCU quarterback Warren Bell (no. 5) goes airborne to avoid colliding with fallen teammate Durant McCathern. (Courtesy of the *Durham Morning Herald*.)

NCCU's Eric Puryear (no. 38) gives Eagle effort in tackling A&T running back Adrian Parks, who rushed for a team-high 47 yards. (Courtesy of the *Durham Morning Herald*.)

Falling again

N.C. Central loses 11th game in a row to North Carolina A&T, this time on a costly turnover that spurs a rout

By MIKE POTTER
mmp@herald-sun.com, 419-6604

Aggie-Eagle Classic	
A&T	40
NCCU	7

Inside/D8

■ Dangerous: This scenario is becoming familiar

RALEIGH — N.C. Central coach Rudy Abrams had said all along that if his football team didn't make mistakes against archrival North Carolina A&T, the Eagles had a chance for an upset.

And it was because they made several big mistakes, not so much because of the Aggies' obvious depth or size, that A&T was a 40-7 winner in the Aggie-Eagle Football Classic on a very wet Sunday night before an announced crowd of 43,134 at N.C. State's Carter-Finley Stadium.

The result in the opener for both teams was the 11th straight win in the series for the Aggies, who are coached by NCCU alumnus and Durham native Billy Hayes. A&T, which is ranked No. 1 nationally in black college football, was ranked in the top 15 of several pre-season Division I-AA polls.

Despite the final margin, fans of the Division II Eagles had to be leaving the stadium shaking their heads and wondering "what if?"

Trailing just 14-7 midway through the third quarter, the Eagles had a third-and-goal at the Aggie 4 when fullback Cheo Johnson was stopped just inches from the goal line. On the next play,

please see CENTRAL/C8

N.C. Central quarterback Warren Bell jumps over teammate Durant McCathern trying to avoid an A&T tackle during the Eagles' loss to the Aggies on Sunday night.

With a 22-point shutout of NCCU in 2001, A&T ran its victory streak to 12 games. A&T's defense dominated, and Maurice Hicks, All-American running back for A&T, broke the game open in the third quarter when he raced 40 yards for a touchdown. Before that play, the Eagles had held Hicks in check. What was a 9-0 A&T lead became 16-0. Hicks finished the game with 58 yards rushing and was named offensive MVP for A&T. A final Aggies touchdown in the fourth quarter sealed the victory. (Courtesy of the *Durham Morning Herald*.)

During the second quarter, Aggies defenders Brad Holmes (no. 95), Asa Evans (no. 29), and Ivan Butler (no. 99) wrap up NCCU running back Montez Patterson behind the line of scrimmage. (Courtesy of the *Durham Morning Herald*.)

A host of Aggies defenders sack NCCU quarterback Lamont Alston (no. 1). (Courtesy of the *News and Observer*.)

Eagles defenders Chris Gilmore (no. 41) and Sheldon Connor (no. 90) tackle A&T's All-American running back Maurice Hicks (no. 22). NCCU's defense held Hicks to 58 yards rushing. (Courtesy of the *News and Observer*.)

In 2002, NCCU came back from a 27-0 first-quarter deficit to defeat A&T in overtime 33-30. The Eagles victory ended Bill Haye's and A&T's win streak at 12 games. A&T started fast, but NCCU finished strong. Nathaniel Fitch caught six passes for 92 yards and two touchdowns for NCCU, but running back Donnie Pippen provided the heroics in overtime when his iconic leaping touchdown from the two yard line sealed the victory for the Eagles. NCCU's Maroon Terror defense played lights out for the remaining three quarters, giving up only six points to the Aggies. But the first quarter was all A&T. In the midst of a swarming Aggie defense that included Charles Parham (32) and Joey Lance (53), A&T's Chamar Milton (43) stripes the ball from NCCU's Sean Williams (11). A&T recovered the fumble. (Courtesy of the *News and Observer*.)

Tailgating is a huge part of the football rivalry. While the game was going on inside the stadium, A&T alumnus Bryan "Ed Mo" Edwards (above) shows off his grill-master skills. His friend and A&T alumnus Larry "Chip" Suitt (left) calls for more Aggie Pride. (Courtesy of the *News and Observer*.)

A&T's Charles Parham provides tight coverage, but NCCU wide receiver Nathaniel Fitch (no. 3) hauls in a touchdown reception. (Courtesy of the *Durham Morning Herald*.)

NCCU's DeLeon Raynor (no. 28) and Jamr Neely (no. 83) leap over A&T's Douglas Brown (no. 5) to recover a fumble. (Courtesy of the *Durham Morning Herald*.)

A REAL CLASSIC

N.C. CENTRAL RALLIES TO FORCE OVERTIME, THEN SHOCKS N.C. A&T

Running back Donnie Pippen soars like an Eagle to score the game-winning touchdown in overtime.

STAFF PHOTOS BY JOHN L. WHITE

The Division II Eagles overcome a 27-0 first-quarter deficit to beat the Aggies after 12 straight losses to their rivals.

After coming back from 27 points down, NCCU running back Donnie Pippen took a handoff from Lawrence Fuller and dove over multiple A&T defenders for the game-winning touchdown. Pippen's heroics ended 12 years of misery for the Eagles. (Courtesy of the *News and Observer*.)

Coach Bill Hayes kept his players on the field for the postgame awards ceremony. Surrounded by despondent but prideful teammates, A&T's Colin Reese (no. 13) dropped his head in disbelief when the championship trophy was given to NCCU. (Courtesy of the *News and Observer*.)

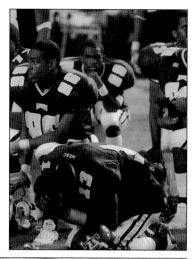

When A&T and Central met in 2003, new coaches were at the helm for both programs. A&T hired George Small to replace Bill Hayes, who was let go at the end of the 2002 season. Small was a former A&T player with NFL playing experience who had spent most of his coaching career as a defensive coordinator but had also been head coach of the Thoroughbreds of Kentucky State University. NCCU chancellor James Ammons hired Bill Hayes to be athletic director, and after coach Rudy Abrams resigned at the end of 2002, Hayes replaced him with Rod Broadway. Broadway had been an assistant coach for 24 years before getting his chance to be a head coach. The Aggies rode a stifling defense and running back Frank Patterson to a 25-0 victory over NCCU in 2003. The Eagles turned the ball over seven times, including five interceptions, and Patterson rushed for 173 yards on 23 carries. The shutout helped A&T avenge the overtime loss to the Eagles from the year before. A&T won the MEAC championship in 2003. Small emphasized defense, and the Aggies went from a 4-3 defense to a 3-4 defense to take advantage of the athleticism of their linebackers. (Courtesy of the *Charlotte Observer*.)

Coach Rod Broadway spent 24 years as an assistant coach before NCCU took a chance on him as a head coach. Broadway had been on coach Steve Spurrier's staff at Duke in 1989, and he changed Central's offense to an aerial attack mixed with running plays. His predecessor Rudy Abrams had run an option offense. (Courtesy of North Carolina Central University Archives–James E. Shepard Memorial Library).)

A&T running back Frank Patterson torched the Eagles for 173 yards rushing. (Courtesy of the *News and Observer*.)

A&T quarterback Marshall Glenn (no. 10) attempts to break free from the clutches of Eagles defender Shamar Robinson (no. 47). (Courtesy of the *News and Observer*.)

Revenge is sweet. A&T defensive coordinator Alonzo Lee and Aggies players celebrate the victory over the Eagles. (Courtesy of the *News and Observer*.)

In 2004, NCCU came into the game feeling confident after defeating Johnson C. Smith 52-0 in the season opener. Both teams played hard-nosed defense, but NCCU's Greg Pruitt Jr. was the game's leading rusher with 110 yards. NCCU stopped A&T on fourth and short with 1:18 left in the fourth quarter, and all they had to do was run the clock out, but on the ensuing first down, NCCU quarterback Adrian Warren fumbled the snap, and A&T's Lammon Ringold recovered the fumble. Aggie nose tackle Brandon Reilford caused the fumble by knocking NCCU's center back when he snapped the ball. A&T won 16-15 after Carlos Davalos kicked a 50-yard game-winning field goal with six seconds left on the clock. Davalos's kick cleared the upright by less than a foot, giving A&T the win. NCCU senior running back, Donnie Pippen, hero of the 2002 come-from-behind monumental upset, had hopes for a victory in his final outing against A&T, but it was not to be. (Courtesy of the *Durham Morning Herald*.)

A&T's Brad Hinton (no. 2) stiff-arms NCCU's Jonathan Sherrill (no. 26). (Courtesy of the *News and Observer*.)

A&T's Jerome Myers (no. 50) comes up to make a stop on NCCU's Greg Pruitt Jr. (no. 34). Pruitt Jr. is NCCU's all-time leading rusher, with 3,008 yards. (Courtesy of the *News and Observer*.)

A&T field goal kicker Carlos Davalos (no. 14) celebrates his game-winning kick with teammates Corey Adderly (no. 74) and Curtis Walls (no. 82). (Courtesy of the *News and Observer*.)

Alone in his thoughts, NCCU's Sean Williams reflects on the loss to A&T. (Courtesy of the *News and Observer*.)

Brothers Maurice and Marshall Glenn competed against each other in the Aggie-Eagle Classic in 2004. Maurice was a senior wide receiver for NCCU, and Marshall was the starting quarterback for A&T. Growing up, the boys were inseparable, including on the gridiron. That changed when Marshall decided to attend A&T rather than follow his older brother to NCCU. Parents Nathaniel and Jacquelyn Glenn are NCCU alums and diehard Eagles. (Courtesy of the *News and Observer*.)

'He tells me how hard he's been practicing, and I tell him how hard I've been working, but we will know who has been when game time comes.'

NCCU'S MAURICE GLENN, ON PREPARING TO PLAY AGAINST HIS BROTHER MARSHALL

The Glenn family talks after NCCU's opener against J.C. Smith; from left, Marshall, Nathaniel, Maurice and Jacquelyn.
STAFF PHOTOS BY TRAVIS LONG

It's brother vs. brother

Maurice and Marshall Glenn on opposite sides of Aggie-Eagle Classic

BY SHEENA JOHNSON
STAFF WRITER

AGGIE-EAGLE CLASSIC

In only its second win versus A&T since 1988 and what turned out to be the final game of the Aggie-Eagle Classic, NCCU pulled out a 23-22 victory over the Aggies in 2005. NCCU's offense exploded for 400 total yards. Quarterback Adrian Warren threw for 269 yards and two touchdowns for the Eagles. Torey Ross had 104 receiving yards for NCCU, and Greg Pruitt Jr. rushed for 131 yards. A&T's Brandon Sweeney was the game's leading rusher, with 151 yards on 32 carries. Scoring between the teams went back and forth until Ross caught a 46-yard touchdown late in the fourth quarter, putting the Eagles up for good. Central went 10-2 on the year, won the CIAA championship, and was named Black College National Champion at the end of the season. Eagles defenders gang-tackle the Aggies ball carrier. (Courtesy of the *News and Observer*.)

NCCU quarterback Adrian Warren (no. 12) passes over an Aggies defender. Warren threw for 269 yards in the game and the game-winning touchdown pass. (Courtesy of the *Charlotte Observer*.)

NCCU wide receiver Torey Ross stiff-arms an Aggies defender to the ground on his way to the game-winning 46-yard touchdown. (Courtesy of the *News and Observer*.)

NCCU players celebrate their victory over A&T. (Courtesy of the *Durham Morning Herald*.)

Chancellor James Ammons hoists the last Aggie-Eagle Classic trophy and celebrates with attorney James "Butch" Williams (right) and Eagles players and fans. (Courtesy of North Carolina Central University Athletics Department.)

NCCU and A&T did not play in 2006, but in Coach Rod Broadway's final year at Central, the Eagles went 11-1 and were the 2006 CIAA Conference and HBCU National Champions. Coach Lee Fobbs was 0-11 in his debut as the Aggies head coach. (Courtesy of Atty. Eric Montgomery.)

EAGLES RULE RIVALRY

Postgame scuffle mars NCCU's win over A&T

27 COLLEGE FOOTBALL 22

N.C. CENTRAL   **N.C. A&T**
4-1   0-4

UP NEXT: vs. Presbyterian
Saturday, 2 p.m.; WJRD 1410-AM

BY MIKE POTTER
mpotter@heraldsun.com; 419-6604

GREENSBORO — It may not have had the designation this time, but once again N.C. Central's game with rival North Carolina A&T was an Aggie-Eagle classic.

It wasn't decided until the Eagles' Eric Ray intercepted a Herb Miller pass at the goal line with 14 seconds left, preserving the Eagles' 27-22 victory on Saturday night at Aggie Stadium.

The minutes after the game were marred by a scuffle after a large group of NCCU players celebrated on the Bulldog logo at midfield and the Aggies strongly objected. But pepper-spray wielding campus police quickly dispersed the mob.

"I'm not happy about what happened at the end — I just didn't like the scene," NCCU coach Mose Rison said.

Said N.C. A&T coach Lee Fobbs: "What happened after the game ended was very unfortunate, and we'll deal with it with our guys. I'm just concerned about our players and our fans. We'll let the powers-that-be deal with it."

But before the postgame disturbance, the Eagles won with defense. Three interceptions, including two returned for touchdowns, helped NCCU (4-1) overcome A&T's 412-199 advantage in total offense.

"Give credit where credit is due," said Rison, the first NCCU coach to win four of his first five games since Larry Little went 4-1 in 1993. "Coach Fobbs and his staff did an outstanding coaching job, and like I said, they were the best football team we've played this season. But I'm extremely proud of my team. We hung in to the bitter end."

Fobbs also gave his team credit for a good effort.

"We had a chance to win the game right up until the finish and played hard on both sides of the ball," Fobbs said. "We were in position to win it, and then [Eric Ray] stepped up and made a great play.

N.C. Central receiver Will Scott (83) celebrates with teammates Saturday night after his first-quarter touchdown reception in the Eagles' victory over N.C. A&T in Greensboro.

THE HERALD-SUN | BERNARD THOMAS

see **NCCU** | page B6

At the end of the 2006 season, Rod Broadway left NCCU to become the head coach at Grambling State University. NCCU hired Moses Rison to replace Broadway. Coach Lee Fobbs Jr. was hired to replace George Small at A&T before the 2006 season, so 2007 was the first year the Fobbs-coached Aggies squared off against the Rison-coached Eagles. With 14 seconds left to go in the game and NCCU leading 27-22, the Eagles' Eric Ray intercepted a Herb Miller pass to seal the victory. For the second year in a row, A&T finished the season with a disappointing 0-11 record. Pictured is the *Herald Sun* article with NCCU wide receiver Will Scott (no. 83) celebrating a first-quarter touchdown with Eagles teammates. (Courtesy of the *Durham Morning Herald*.)

In 2008, the teams played at Memorial Stadium in Charlotte, and NCCU defeated A&T 28-27, the third game decided by one point in the previous four games and NCCU's third win in a row. Relying on the quarterback play of Stratford Brown and ball carrying of Tim Shankle, Central got out to a 21-0 lead in the second quarter before A&T made a comeback. The Aggies knocked Stradford out of the game with a broken collarbone while climbing back into the game. In the third quarter, with the score 21-13 for NCCU, Eagles linebacker Alex Winters picked up an Aggies fumble and returned it 38 yards for a touchdown and a 28-13 lead. A&T running back Nigel Tomlin scored on a 21-yard run in the third quarter to cut the lead to 28-20 and on a one-yard run in the fourth to bring the Aggies to within two, but Lee Fobbs elected to kick the extra point rather than go for two, and that ended up being the difference in the game. After losing 28 of 30 games, A&T let go of Fobbs in late October, and assistant coach George Ragsdale took over on an interim basis. Pictured are Eagles defenders tackling A&T's Dione McNair (no. 28). (Courtesy of the *Charlotte Observer*.)

NCCU's Will Scott (no. 83) makes a diving reception over a couple of Aggies. (Courtesy of the *Charlotte Observer*.)

In 2009, Alonzo Lee, longtime defensive coach for A&T, debuted in the rivalry as a head coach, and A&T ended NCCU's three-game win streak with a 23-17 double-overtime victory. A&T quarterback Carlton Fears lobbed a 24-yard touchdown pass to Wallace Miles for the win in the second overtime. Fears passed for 166 yards on eight completions, finishing the game as A&T's leading rusher with 58 yards. Will Scott was almost the difference for NCCU; the Eagles receiver finished the game with a career-high 179 yards receiving, including a 73-yard touchdown pass from Michael Johnson. But A&T's defense was stingy and picked off Johnson three times and forced him to fumble once. (Courtesy of the *Clarion Ledger*.)

Aggies edge Eagles in 2nd OT

THE HERALD-SUN | CODEY JOHNSON

C. Central's Will Scott heads to the end zone for a
irth-quarter touchdown on a pass from Michael John-
against N.C. A&T on Saturday night in Greensboro.

BY BRIAN HENDRICKSON
Special to The Herald-Sun

GREENSBORO — N.C. Central rallied from a big de
icit in spite of numerous turnovers and mistake
that nearly let the game get away early.

And that's part of what made the ending o
Saturday's game against North Carolina A&T s
heartbreaking.

After rallying to tie the game with 17 unan
swered points, the Eagles had a field goal blocke
in overtime before giving up a 24-yard touchdow
pass in the second overtime to fall 23-17 to Nort
Carolina A&T at Aggie Stadium. The loss break
NCCU's three-game winning streak agains th
Aggies.

"I thought we made a lot of awful mistakes,
said NCCU coach Mose Rison, who pointed to th
Eagles' seven penalties that cost 121 yards —
many coming at crucial points in the game — a
a reason for the loss. "I talk to them about thing
you can do and can't do, especially in a game o
this magnitude. We shouldn't have been in tha
situation."

The Eagles already had dodged chances to le
the game slip away. Patrick Courtney missed
36-yard field goal with six seconds remainin
that would have given N.C. A&T the lead, the
missed his third of the game on the openin
drive of overtime. But the blocked field goal i

see **NCCU** | page B5

A&T proved too much for the Eagles, who made a late push but came up short. (Courtesy of the
Durham Morning Herald.)

After a 30-year hiatus, in 2010, NCCU returned to the NCAA Division I-AA level and rejoined the MEAC, a league it had helped to form in 1970 and began playing football in 1971. In large part because of seven A&T turnovers, the Eagles won 27-16 in front of the largest crowd to see a football game on NCCU's campus. It was also the first time the teams played in Durham since 1992, when A&T trounced the Eagles 49-7. Off Aggies turnovers, Central jumped out to a 21-0 lead and then held off the Aggies for the victory. NCCU's senior running back, Tim Shankle, rushed for 86 yards, enough to push him over 2,000 yards for his career. Eagles linebacker Donald Laster recovered two fumbles in the first quarter, resulting in Central touchdowns. A&T running back Mark Mayhew starred for the Aggies by rushing for 183 yards and scoring a touchdown. At the end of 2010, NCCU moved on from coach Mose Rison and replaced him with Henry Frazier III. Rison did not win enough at NCCU, but he went 3-1 against A&T. A&T canned coach Alonzo Lee during the season, and George Ragsdale finished the season as interim head coach. NCCU's Marc Lewis (no. 25) gets assistance from teammate Ja'Quez Canty (no. 27) in taking down A&T wide receiver Wallace Miles (no. 8). (Courtesy of the *Durham Morning Herald*.)

Before the 2011 season, NCA&T and NCCU got new head coaches. A&T hired coach Rod Broadway for the Aggies football program. Broadway came to A&T fresh from reviving the Grambling Tigers football machine, where he won a Black College National Championship in 2008. The 2011 Aggie-Eagle match-up pitted two former SWAC and Black College National Champion coaches against each other. Broadway's Aggies bested Frazier's Eagles by a score of 31-21 in their first meeting. A&T running back Mike Mayhew was the best player on the field for a second year in a row, rushing for an impressive 163 yards for the Aggies. A&T wide receiver Wallace Miles was also impressive. He caught eight passes for 123 yards and a touchdown. A&T jumped out to a 14-0 lead and never trailed in the game played at home. NCCU chancellor Charlie Nelms (left) places an Eagles baseball cap on the head of new head football coach Henry Frazier III (right). In December 2010, coach Frazer came to NCCU from Prairie View State University, where he went 43-30 and was credited with reviving one of the most moribund athletic teams in HBCU history. Before Frazier arrived at Prairie View and got the Panthers on the winning side of the ledger, their most recent winning season was 1976. Frazier had also been a head coach at Bowie State University in Maryland. (Courtesy of the *Durham Morning Herald*.)

In this A&T yearbook photograph, linebacker Devin Ray (no. 52), defensive end Tony Mashburn (no. 54), and teammates get ready to spring into action against the visiting Eagles. (Courtesy of DigitalNC.org Yearbook Online Archive.)

In 2012, A&T running back Mike Mayhew scored the game-winning touchdown in overtime to defeat NCCU in Durham 22-16. Mayhew rushed for 116 yards. A&T held NCCU to 46 yards rushing and forced six fumbles. Eagles linebacker Ty Brown (no. 6) and Aggies fullback Devon Moore (no. 45) share a few kind words during the game. (Courtesy of North Carolina Central University Athletics Department.)

A&T's Jose Garcia-Camacho (no. 38) looks on while coach Rod Broadway receives a Gatorade bath and Aggies players, including Tony Clodfelter (no. 57) and Tyree Andrews (no. 30), celebrate the win over NCCU. (Courtesy of DigitalNC.org Yearbook Online Archive.)

In shutting out NCCU 28-0 in 2013, A&T ran its win streak over the Eagles to three games. Mike Mayhew graduated in 2012, and Tarik Cohen took over ball-carrying duties for the Aggies. In his first game against the Eagles, Cohen rushed for 125 yards on 31 carries, but the Aggie defense was the most impressive. NCCU managed only 35 yards through the air and just 109 yards rushing. A&T quarterback Lewis Kindle opened the scoring for the Aggies with a one-yard touchdown. Ricky Lewis also scored on a one-yard run. A&T defenders also scored touchdowns off of an interception and fumble. In 2013, coach Dwayne Foster served as interim head coach for the Eagles, and because of ongoing personal challenges that were interfering with his role as head coach, Central terminated coach Henry Frazier III at the end of the season. A&T running back Tarik Cohen (no. 28) weaves through Eagle defenders, Travis McCorkle (no. 91) and Felix Small (no. 42). As a freshman in 2013, Cohen finished the season with 1,148 yards rushing. Easily one of the most dynamic players in the history of the MEAC, Cohen set the all-time rushing record for A&T and the MEAC while also leading the Aggies to the 2015 HBCU Championship. (Courtesy of Dr. Michael Simmons.)

In 2014, NCCU defeated A&T in Durham 21-14, and both teams earned a share of the MEAC Championship. The teams were notched at 7-7 coming out of halftime, but behind the quarterback play of Malcolm Bell and the rushing of Andre Clark, the Eagles put together a six-play, 84-yard scoring drive that gave NCCU a 7-point advantage. A costly A&T miscue gave the Eagles the ball at the Aggies' 37, and Malcolm Bell ran it in from there, making it 21-7 NCCU in the third quarter. Tarik Coken was unstoppable for A&T. He rushed for 203 yards and averaged 10 yards per carry. Cohen scored late in the third quarter, but the NCCU Maroon Terror defense shut out the Aggies in the fourth quarter to seal the victory. In 2014, NCCU athletic director Dr. Ingrid Wicker-McCree (left) hired Jerry Mack (center) to be the next head coach of NCCU. Coach Mark recalled that during his interview, Chancellor Debra Saunders-White (right) asked how he would fix the Eagles' Red Zone scoring issues. He indicated that her support of the team was important to their success. Mack was 33 when he was hired and came to the Eagles from South Alabama, where he was wide receivers coach. He had previous assistant coaching stints at Jackson State, Central Arkansas, Arkansas–Pine Bluff, and Memphis. (Courtesy of the *News and Observer*.)

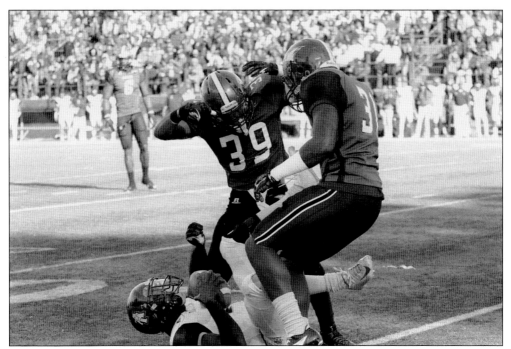

NCCU defensive back Sayyid Muhammad (no. 39) and linebacker Tre Smith (no. 31) stand over Aggies quarterback Kwashaun Quick (no. 2). (Courtesy of North Carolina Central University Athletics Department.)

Eagles running back Deyonta Wright (no. 28) attempts to outpace diving Aggies linebacker D'vonte Grant (no. 4). (Courtesy of North Carolina Central University Athletics Department.)

In 2015, for the second year in a row, NCCU defeated A&T and the teams were cochampions of the MEAC. NCCU quarterback Malcolm Bell threw for 200 yards and ran for a touchdown. With Central leading 14-10 in the fourth quarter, Eagles running back Dorrel McClain broke the game open when he scored on a 16-yard run. McClain was the game's leading rusher with 167 yards on 20 carries. A&T's Tarik Cohen carried the ball 22 times for 123 yards. Each team had a special teams touchdown in the first half. In the second quarter, NCCU's LaVontis Smith scored on a 67-yard punt return. Smith also had 123 yards receiving. Not to be outdone, on the ensuing kick-off, Aggies return man Tony McRae took the kick back for a 90-yard touchdown. A&T attended the inaugural Celebration Bowl and defeated Alcorn State University to win the Black College National Championship. NCCU quarterback Malcolm Bell (no. 15) dives over Aggies linebacker Leroy Hill (no. 54) for a first down. Aggies defensive end Angelo Keyes (no. 50) is also pictured. (Courtesy of the *Charlotte Observer.*)

With the Aggies in pursuit, NCCU running back Dorrel McClain points to the sky as he heads for a 16-yard touchdown run in the fourth quarter. (Courtesy of North Carolina Central University Athletics Department.)

After preventing a reception by A&T wide receiver Denzel Keyes (no. 1), NCCU linebacker Jordan Miles (no. 10) congratulates teammates Ryan Smith (no. 2) and C.J. Moore (no. 32), who celebrate with a high five. Also pictured is NCCU defensive lineman Tre Smith (no. 31). (Courtesy of North Carolina Central University Athletics Department.)

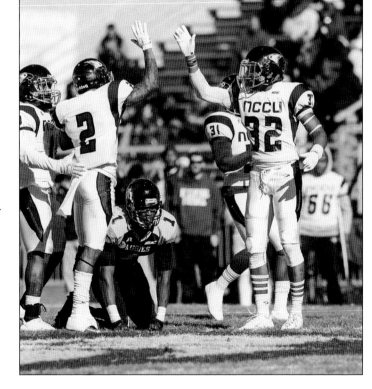

On the stellar quarterback play of Malcolm Bell, NCCU throttled A&T 42-21 in Durham and three-peated as MEAC champions, winning the conference title outright in 2016. After a scoreless first quarter, NCCU scored the first 21 points and never allowed the Aggies to get going. Bell passed for 184 yards and rushed for 131 yards in the victory. Dorrel McClain scored three touchdowns. The longest was a 76-yard run in the fourth quarter. The victory allowed NCCU to represent the MEAC in the Celebration Bowl against Grambling State University. NCCU linebacker Jeremy Miles (no. 11) celebrates a big play for the Eagles. Teammate Roderick "Dee" Harris is pictured in the background. A&T's Josh Mattocks (no. 61), Anthony McMinn II (no. 36), and Xavier Griffin (no. 3) are also pictured. (Courtesy of North Carolina Central University Athletics Department.)

Malcolm Bell (no. 15), the Eagles quarterback, takes off for a 41-yard touchdown run in the second quarter of the game. Aggie Tard McCoy (no. 5) and a teammate (no. 9) chase Bell. (Courtesy of North Carolina Central University Athletics Department.)

Khalil Stinson (no. 6) brings in a one-handed reception for the Eagles over A&T defensive back Marquis Willis (no. 32). (Courtesy of North Carolina Central University Athletics Department.)

A&T linebacker Jeremy Taylor (no. 48) stares back at an NCCU player. Also pictured is A&T defensive back Marquis Willis (no. 32). (Courtesy of North Carolina Central University Athletics Department.)

In 2017, Rod Broadway and A&T defeated NCCU 24-10 on their way to going 12-0, receiving a second Celebration Bowl berth and eventually defeating Grambling State University to win another Black College National Championship. Lamar Raynard, A&T's quarterback, passed for 153 yards and a touchdown. Raynard also rushed for 40 yards. Aggie running back Jamari Smith led all rushers with 99 yards on 14 carries. A&T opened the scoring when Raynard connected with Elijah Bell on a 13-yard touchdown reception. Marquell Cartwright scored two touchdowns on short runs for the Aggies. Each team kicked a field goal. NCCU's lone touchdown came on a three-yard run by Isaiah Totten. Coach Jerry Mack resigned as coach of the Eagles after the season, and Granville Eastman took his place on an interim basis. Rod Broadway is one of the greatest HBCU football coaches of all time. He won five national championships across three HBCUs: NCCU, Grambling, and A&T. NCCU took a chance on Broadway when they hired him in 2003, because he had never before been a head coach at the collegiate level. While at Central from 2003 to 2006, Broadway made the most of his opportunity. He won two CIAA and two national championships. He won at Grambling State, his next stop, before becoming the head coach of A&T in 2011. He remained at A&T through 2017 and built the Aggies into a juggernaut. A&T won a share of the MEAC title in 2014 and 2015, and they won it outright in 2017, and Broadway led the Aggies to national championships in 2015 and 2017. (Courtesy of the *Winston-Salem Journal*.)

A&T quarterback Lamar Raynard (no. 7) outraces Eagle defenders. He led the Aggies to back-to-back MEAC and Black College National Championships in 2017 and 2018. Raynard is the Aggies' all-time passing leader in passing yards and touchdowns. (Courtesy of Kevin L. Dorsey Photography.)

Aggies head coach Rod Broadway (right) looks on as A&T wide receiver Elijah Bell (no. 13) makes a one-handed reception over NCCU defensive back Alphonso Carter (no. 23). (Courtesy of HBCUSports.com.)

The NCCU offensive line, including Nick Leverett (no. 75), Stewart Boyd (no. 60), Andrew Dale (no. 70), and Marley Conley (no. 74), pass protect with assistance from running back Isaiah Totten (no. 25). (Courtesy of North Carolina Central University Athletics Department.)

In 2018, Sam Washington replaced Rod Broadway as head coach of A&T, and the Aggies dominated NCCU from start to finish. The game was never competitive, and A&T won 45-0. NCCU gained 21 yards rushing and had 41 yards of total offense, while A&T amassed 539 yards of total offense. A&T scored twice in each of the first three quarters. Lamar Raynard, the A&T quarterback, opened the scoring with a four-yard pass to Elijah Bell in the first quarter. Aggies running back Marquell Cartwright scored on a 35-yard touchdown run later in the first quarter. After an Aggies field goal in the second quarter, Jah-Maine Martin got on the board with a 10-yard touchdown run. Cartwright scored on a short run in the third quarter, and Raynard found Bell again, this time for a 24-yard touchdown pass. Kashon Baker closed out the scoring for A&T with a one-yard run in the fourth quarter. A&T won the MEAC for the second year in a row and defeated Alcorn State University in the Celebration Bowl to win the Black College National Championship. The Aggies also won the Black College National Championship in 2019. A&T head coach Sam Washington was a defensive coordinator at NCCU from 1993 to 2000. In 2022, A&T let Washington go. (Courtesy of the Ultimaterecruits.com.)

In 2019, Dr. Ingrid Wicker-McCree hired Trei Oliver to be the Eagles' next head coach. Sam Washington and the Aggies gave Oliver a rude welcome to the rivalry—the 54-0 victory is the largest in the history of the series. A&T held Central to nine yards total offense while gaining 520 yards; 343 were rushing yards. Jah-Maine Martin and Kashon Baker each scored two rushing touchdowns, and quarterback Kylil Carter threw a pair of touchdowns. Trei Oliver played safety for NCCU from 1994 to 1997. His father, Colon Oliver, played defensive back for the Eagles from 1963 to 1966. Coach Oliver (center) came to NCCU after being the defensive coordinator for the Jaguars of Southern University (2016–2019). Before that, he coached linebackers on Rod Broadway's staff at A&T (2011–2015). (Courtesy of North Carolina Central University Archives–James E. Shepard Memorial Library.)

Aggies linebacker Antoine Wilder (no. 9) lines up for a tackle on NCCU running back Isaiah Totten (no. 25). (Courtesy HBCU Sports.com)

The COVID-19 pandemic caused the cancellation of the 2020 football season for A&T and NCCU. In 2021, A&T and NCCU played in Greensboro, and the Aggies defeated the Eagles 37-14. A&T built a 21-3 halftime lead behind the running of Kashon Baker, who ended the day with 137 yards, including a 47-yard run and a rushing touchdown. Contrarily, Central never got its ground game going, ending the day with 52 total yards rushing. NCCU had more success through the air. Eagles quarterback Davius Richard completed 21 passes for 225 yards, a touchdown, and an interception. He also rushed for 29 yards. Ryan McDaniel, a senior wide receiver for NCCU, had a game- and career-high 178 yards receiving, including a 77-yard reception. McDaniel also had a receiving touchdown. A&T kicked a field goal in the third quarter to increase its lead to 30-3. NCCU kicked a field goal and scored a touchdown in the fourth quarter. A&T closed out the scoring with a touchdown with 1:20 left in the game. NCCU defensive back Travon Wallace (no. 16) leaps high to block Andrew Brown's (no. 39) field goal attempt. (Courtesy of *North Carolina Central University Campus Echo*.)

A&T defenders gang-tackle NCCU running back Isaiah Totten (no. 25). (Courtesy of Kevin L. Dorsey Photography.)

A&T's Miles Simon (no. 4) prepares to tackle Ryan McDaniel (no. 15), who had a game-high 178 yards receiving, which was also a career-best for the senior Eagles wide receiver. (Courtesy of North Carolina Central University Athletics Department.)

Played in Charlotte, the 2022 game marked the 100th anniversary of the football rivalry. The teams first played in Greensboro in 1922. In 2022, head coach Tre Oliver led his Eagles to a 28-13 victory over A&T. Eagles quarterback and captain Davius Richard was the difference in the game for NCCU, accounting for all of NCCU's points. The junior quarterback from Belle Glade, Florida, rushed for 54 yards and two touchdowns and passed for 200 yards and two touchdowns. Richard completed passes to eight different teammates, including E.J. Hicks and Kyle Morgan, who had touchdown receptions. A&T quarterback Zach Yeager threw for 275 yards, a touchdown, and an interception. Yeager also rushed for 59 yards. Central dominated the time of possession. The Eagles held the ball for 34:53, compared to A&T's 25:07. Neither team got much going on the ground, but NCCU converted third downs 62 percent of the time, compared to 40 percent for A&T. Richard led NCCU on a 12-play, 65-yard touchdown to start the scoring. Yeager responded for A&T with a 55-yard touchdown pass to Jamison Warren later in the first quarter. But the Aggies could only manage two field goals for the remainder of the game. Those came in the second quarter. NCCU scored two touchdowns in the second quarter and one in the third to close the scoring. The final touchdown was a 16-yard pass from Richard to Hicks. The Eagles (above) celebrate a touchdown on the opening drive. (Courtesy of Douglas Burt Photography.)

Aggies defensive end Janorris Robertson (no. 91) hangs on to Eagles running back Latrell Collier (no. 5), who gets behind the block of offensive lineman Robert Mitchell (no. 55). (Courtesy of HBCUSports.com.)

Junior NCCU defensive back Kalil Baker (no. 20) celebrates an interception with teammates JaJuan Hudson (No. 7), Albert Reid (no. 44), and Marseille Miller (no. 80). (Courtesy of Douglas Burt Photography.)

Elliot Kadans (no. 49) held for placekicker Andrew Brown (no. 39), who nailed a career-long 49-yard field goal at the end of the first half. (Courtesy of Kevin L. Dorsey Photography.)

NCCU tight end Tyler Barnes (no. 81) celebrates while offensive lineman Corey Bullock (no. 51) embraces Kyle Serba, deputy athletic director for external affairs. Serba has been at NCCU since 1994. (Courtesy of the *Durham Morning Herald*.)

NCCU quarterback Davius Richard (no. 11), linebacker Corey Patterson (no. 49), offensive lineman Chris Escalera (no. 70), and Eagle teammates celebrate the historic win over A&T. In 2022, Richard led the Eagles to a share of the conference title and a Black College National Championship over previously undefeated Jackson State in the Celebration Bowl. (Courtesy of Douglas Burt Photography.)

The NCCU Eagles, champions of the Duke Mayo Classic, pause for a team photograph after the victory over rival North Carolina A&T State University. (Courtesy of North Carolina Central University Athletics Department.)

Aggie Pride is real, and the eight-time Black College National Champion North Carolina A&T State University Aggies will be looking to climb back on top of NCCU in 2023 and the years ahead. This is a photo of the A&T team for 2022. (Courtesy of Kevin L. Dorsey Photography.)

In a physical and determined run that summed up the play of the Eagles in the victory over previously unbeaten Jackson State, NCCU running back Latrell Collier (no. 5) stiff arms Cam'Ron Silmon-Craig (no. 7) and brash Coach Deon Sanders's championship hopes to the turf. (Courtesy of North Carolina Central University Athletics Department.)

NCCU began the 100th anniversary of the football rivalry with a remarkable win over A&T to start the season and finished the season by running over undefeated Jackston State in the Celebration Bowl. Posing with the Celebration Bowl championship trophy were offensive MVP Davius Richard (left); defensive MVP Khalil Baker; NCCU chancellor Dr. Johnson O'Akinyele; athletic director Louis "Skip" Perkins; Yvette Oliver, wife of coach Trei Oliver; coach Trei Oiver embracing his parents, Evelyn and Colon Oliver; and George "Bulldog" Smith, senior associate athletic director for external affairs and director of strength and conditioning (right). (Courtesy of North Carolina Central University Athletics Department.)

CONCLUSION

This volume honors the coaches, players, bands, cheerleaders, alumni, and fans of this historic rivalry. North Carolina Agricultural & Technical State University (A&T) and North Carolina Central University (NCCU) played for the first time on November 23, 1922, in Greensboro. For 100 years, the schools have battled on the gridiron. NCAT leads the 92-game series 52-35-5, but the series lead belies the average game score difference of only eight points. It might surprise some Aggies that Coach Bill Hayes, NCAT's all-time winningest coach and the coach who won the most games in the rivalry, is an alumnus of NCCU. It might surprise some Eagles to know that after Coach Herman Riddick, NCCU player's favorite was Coach Robert "Stonewall" Jackson, a proud 1950 graduate of NCAT. Bill Hayes was merciless against the Eagles, and Jackson made every effort to defeat NCAT. Such are the contradictions that exist in the rivalry.

Lopsided winning streaks defined the games played In the 1920s and the 1930s. The Aggies won the first four games, and the teams tied once. NCCU won the next four games between 1930 and 1933, such that in 1934 both teams had a 4-4-1 record in the series. The Eagles did not win another game until 1941, but an ineligible player cost them that game. NCAT's Lonnie P. Byarm and NCCU's Wilson Vashon Eagleson were the first coaches to coach in the rivalry. NCAT joined the Colored Intercollegiate Athletic Association (CIAA) in 1924, and NCCU followed in 1928. NCAT won its first conference title in 1927. NCC won its first in 1941, only to see it given to Morgan State over the ineligible player.

In many ways, the period 1940 to 1959 was a high water mark for the teams and the rivalry. Both teams had future Hall of Fame coaches and rosters with future professional players. Because of racial segregation, most of the best African American football players in North Carolina were on the rosters of NCC and A&T.

The 1960 to 1979 era of the rivalry coincided with the modern Civil Rights Movement and the integration of higher education and collegiate football. Before the 1970s, the top African American high school football players in the state played for A&T and NCC, but with the acceleration of racial integration of many predominantly white universities, especially after 1970, these players increasingly attended historically white schools. In 1971, NCC and A&T left the (CIAA) and became charter members of the Mid-Eastern Athletic Conference (MEAC). Between 1960 and 1974, NCC won ten out of fifteen games and experienced its greatest success in the rivalry. But beginning in 1975, A&T turned the tables and won four out of the last five games of the era.

Through the 1980s and into the 1990s, the rivalry between the Aggies and the Eagles rose to a fever pitch, and many records were set on the field of play. In 1980, NCC returned to the CIAA, which played at the NCAA Division II level. A&T remained in the MEAC at the Division I-AA level. As a Division II program, NCC had less than half the number of scholarship football players as A&T. Beginning in 1994, the games were played at Carter Finley Stadium in Raleigh as the Aggie-Eagle Classic. A&T dominated that Classic. Yet, in spite of being in a lower division, the Eagles won four games to A&T's 6 in the 1980s. The teams tied in 1983. A&T dominated the 1990s.

The new millennium ushered in an era of changes and excitement for the rivalry as both programs achieved unparalleled success on the gridiron. The long-running Aggie-Eagle Classic ended in 2005. Also crucial to the series, NCCU returned to the MEAC in 2010, moving from NCAA Division II to Division I. This significantly increased the number of scholarships available for the football team.

Both teams won multiple conference and national championships in this period. From 2014 to 2019, A&T was at the top of the MEAC standings every year except 2016, when NCCU was the undisputed conference champion. NCCU had a share of the conference crown in 2014 and 2015. Rod Broadway led NCCU to HBCU Championships in 2005 and 2006. Jerry Mack was a costly penalty away from winning the national championship in 2016. A&T went on a title run for the ages by winning four national championships in five years: 2015, 2017, 2018, and 2019. Coach

Rod Broadway was the head coach for the first two, and Sam Washington coached the Aggies for the second two.

Most recently, Coach Trei Oliver, a former Eagle player whose father, Colon, also played for NCC, led the Eagles to an upset victory over previously unbeaten Jackson State University led by brash coach Deon Sanders or "Coach Prime." For their outstanding play, NCCU quarterback Davius Richard and defensive back Khalil Baker were named Offensive MVP and Defensive MVP, respectively, of the Celebration Bowl.

After 100 years of competition, the rivalry remains strong, and interest in the game remains high. A&T leads the overall record between the two schools, 54-34-5. There are seven years when the schools did not play football: 1923, 1926, 1929, 1943, 1944, 1993, and 2006. A&T has moved to the Coastal Athletic Association (CAA), but the rivalry shows no signs of losing intensity. It embodies the passion-filled pride, commitment to excellence, and unquenchable spirit of determination that characterize both institutions and set them apart from their peers. With all of its intensity, the rivalry also defines what it truly means to be an Aggie or an Eagle. Iron sharpens iron, and for the next 100 years, Aggies and Eagles will continue to give each other the business, thus preparing each other to dominate the rest!

Even in recent years, Randolph Henderson and Roosevelt Pratt continue to display the pride and spirit of camaraderie that the Aggie-Eagle rivalry embodies. (Courtesy of Roosevelt Pratt.)

Table of Games

Date	Location	Winner	Score
November 23, 1922	Greensboro	North Carolina A&T	26–0
1923	Teams Did Not Play		
November 22, 1924	Durham	Tie	13–13
October 24, 1925	Greensboro	North Carolina A&T	19–0
1926	Teams Did Not Play		
October 22, 1927	Greensboro	North Carolina A&T	28–13
October 13, 1928	Winston-Salem	North Carolina A&T	20–0
1929	Teams Did Not Play		
November 1, 1930	Durham	North Carolina Central	20–14
October 31, 1931	Durham	North Carolina Central	6–0
November 24, 1932	Greensboro	North Carolina Central	19–0
November 30, 1933	Durham	North Carolina Central	20–0
November 29, 1934	Greensboro	North Carolina A&T	6–0
November 30, 1935	Durham	North Carolina A&T	9–0†

† A&T forfeited game with NCC because of an ineligible player.

Date	Location	Winner	Score
November 26, 1936	Greensboro	North Carolina A&T	39–0
November 25, 1937	Durham	North Carolina A&T	14–7
November 24, 1938	Greensboro	North Carolina A&T	25–0
November 30, 1939	Durham	North Carolina A&T	7–0
November 28, 1940	Greensboro	North Carolina A&T	12–6
November 22, 1941	Durham	North Carolina Central	9–6††

†† NCC forfeited game with A&T and the CIAA title because of an ineligible player.

Date	Location	Winner	Score
November 26, 1942	Greensboro	North Carolina Central	16–12
1943	Teams Did Not Play		
1944	Teams Did Not Play		
October 20, 1945	Durham	North Carolina Central	40–0
October 19, 1946	Greensboro	North Carolina A&T	17–0
December 6, 1947	Durham	North Carolina Central	17–0
December 4, 1948	Greensboro	Tie	6–6
November 24, 1949	Greensboro	North Carolina A&T	33–6
November 23, 1950	Durham	North Carolina A&T	25–13
November 22, 1951	Greensboro	North Carolina A&T	13–6
November 27, 1952	Durham	North Carolina A&T	26–0
November 26, 1953	Greensboro	North Carolina Central	15–6
November 25, 1954	Durham	North Carolina Central	7–6
November 24, 1955	Greensboro	Tie	7–7
November 22, 1956	Durham	North Carolina Central	20–0
November 28, 1957	Greensboro	North Carolina A&T	21–0
November 27, 1958	Durham	North Carolina A&T	20–18
November 26, 1959	Greensboro	North Carolina A&T	3–0
November 24, 1960	Greensboro	North Carolina Central	14–13
November 23, 1961	Durham	North Carolina Central	13–0
November 17, 1962	Durham	North Carolina A&T	28–7
November 28, 1963	Greensboro	North Carolina Central	6–0
November 26, 1964	Durham	North Carolina A&T	46–0
November 25, 1965	Greensboro	North Carolina Central	7–6
November 24, 1966	Durham	North Carolina Central	12–6
November 23, 1967	Greensboro	North Carolina A&T	19–6
November 27, 1968	Durham	North Carolina A&T	21–6

November 22, 1969	Greensboro	Tie	28–28
November 21, 1970	Durham	North Carolina Central	13–7
November 20, 1971	Greensboro	North Carolina Central	14–13
November 18, 1972	Durham	North Carolina Central	9–7
November 17, 1973	Greensboro	North Carolina Central	16–6
November 23, 1974	Durham	North Carolina Central	29–18
November 22, 1975	Greensboro	North Carolina A&T	34–16
November 20, 1976	Durham	North Carolina Central	17–16
November 19, 1977	Greensboro	North Carolina A&T	25–6
November 18, 1978	Durham	North Carolina A&T	17–13
November 17, 1979	Greensboro	North Carolina A&T	23–20
November 22, 1980	Durham	North Carolina A&T	49–13
December 13, 1980	Richmond, VA	North Carolina A&T	37–0
November 28, 1981	Greensboro	North Carolina Central	35–7
November 13, 1982	Durham	North Carolina A&T	13–7
November 12, 1983	Greensboro	Tie	13–13
November 10, 1984	Durham	North Carolina Central	49–10
November 16, 1985	Greensboro	North Carolina A&T	28–19
November 15, 1986	Durham	North Carolina A&T	35–12
November 14, 1987	Greensboro	North Carolina Central	38–19
September 3, 1988	Durham	North Carolina Central	15–2
September 2, 1989	Greensboro	North Carolina A&T	24–6
September 1, 1990	Charlotte	North Carolina A&T	21–6
September 7, 1991	Greensboro	North Carolina A&T	48–0
September 5, 1992	Greensboro	North Carolina A&T	49–7
1993	Teams Did Not Play		
September 3, 1994	Raleigh	North Carolina A&T	38–9
September 3, 1995	Raleigh	North Carolina A&T	18–17
August 31, 1996	Raleigh	North Carolina A&T	38–31 OT
August 30, 1997	Raleigh	North Carolina A&T	36–7
September 5, 1998	Raleigh	North Carolina A&T	40–10
September 5, 1999	Raleigh	North Carolina A&T	20–7
September 3, 2000	Raleigh	North Carolina A&T	40–7
September 1, 2001	Raleigh	North Carolina A&T	22–0
September 1, 2002	Raleigh	North Carolina Central	33–30 OT
August 31, 2003	Raleigh	North Carolina A&T	25–0
September 5, 2004	Raleigh	North Carolina A&T	16–15
September 5, 2005	Raleigh	North Carolina Central	23–22
2006	Teams Did Not Play		
September 22, 2007	Greensboro	North Carolina Central	27–22
October 4, 2008	Charlotte	North Carolina Central	28–27
October 3, 2009	Greensboro	North Carolina A&T	23–17 2OT
September 25, 2010	Durham	North Carolina Central	27–16
November 19, 2011	Greensboro	North Carolina A&T	31–21
November 18, 2012	Durham	North Carolina A&T	22–16 OT
November 23, 2013	Greensboro	North Carolina A&T	28–0
November 22, 2014	Durham	North Carolina Central	21–14
November 21, 2015	Greensboro	North Carolina Central	21–16
November 19, 2016	Durham	North Carolina Central	42–21
November 18, 2017	Greensboro	North Carolina A&T	24–10
November 17, 2018	Durham	North Carolina A&T	45–0
November 23, 2019	Greensboro	North Carolina A&T	54–0
2020	Teams Did Not Play		
September 25, 2021	Greensboro	North Carolina A&T	37–14
September 4, 2022	Charlotte	North Carolina Central	28–13

BIBLIOGRAPHY

ARCHIVAL COLLECTIONS

Durham Herald Co. Newspaper Photographic Collection, c. 1945–2002. North Carolina Collection Photographic Archives. University of North Carolina at Chapel Hill. finding-aids.lib.unc.edu/P0105/

Historic NCAT vs. NCCU game footage, Aggie Video Archive, F.D. Bluford Library, North Carolina Agricultural and Technical State University, Greensboro, NC.

DIGITAL COLLECTIONS

Aggie Digital Collections and Scholarship, F.D. Bluford Library, North Carolina Agricultural and Technical State University, Greensboro, NC. digital.library.ncat.edu/mlncat/

North Carolina Agricultural and Technical State University Football Story Archive. ncataggies.com/sports/football/archives?page=19

North Carolina Central University Central Intercollegiate Athletic Association and Other Athletics Records, 1915–2009. University Archives, Records and History Center in the James E. Shepard Memorial Library, North Carolina Central University.

North Carolina Central University, Digital Sports Archive. nccueaglepride.com/sports/football

North Carolina Yearbooks, DigitalNC. www.digitalnc.org/collections/yearbooks

PROQUEST HISTORICAL NEWSPAPERS: BLACK NEWSPAPERS COLLECTION

Afro-American (Baltimore, MD)
Greensboro Daily News (Greensboro, NC)
Norfolk Journal and Guide (Norfolk, VA)
Pittsburgh Courier (Pittsburgh, PA)

DIGITAL NC: NEWSPAPERS ONLINE

Campus Echo (NCCU)
Carolinian (Raleigh, NC)
Carolina Times (Durham, NC)
Charlotte Observer (Charlotte, NC)
News and Record (Greensboro, NC)
Register (NCA&T)
Durham Herald (Durham, NC)
New York Amsterdam News (New York, NY)
News and Observer (Raleigh, NC)
Seattle Times (Seattle, WA)

YEARBOOKS

Ayantee. North Carolina Agricultural and Technical State University, Greensboro, NC.
Eagle. North Carolina Central University, Durham, NC.

WEBSITES

HBCU Game Day. hbcugameday.com/2017/11/20/aggie-eagle-classic/

John Barbee
Frank Battle
Connie Boykin
Coach Rod Broadway
Ernest Brown
Ann Reyna Bryson
Hon. G. K. Butterfield
Xavier Cason
James Devone
Alan Fitzgerald
William Fitzgerald
Stanley Gibbs
Antonio Gray
Dr. Jim C. Harper
Coach Bill Hayes
Dr. Jerry Head
Delbert Jarmon
Coach Adrian Jones
Alexander Jones
Edwin Jones
Atty. Kristi Jones
Charles Knox
Harrison Lyon
Coach Jerry Mack
Peter Mason
Dr. Ingrid Wicker McCree
Hon. H.M. "Mickey" Michaux
June Williams Michaux
Atty. Eric Montgomery
Hon. Elaine O'Neal
Billy Reid
James Robbins
Travis Smith
Donald Thomas
Kay Thomas
Hon. George Wallace
Mary "Little Rah Rah!" Wallace
Floyd Wicker
Lisa Wilder
Faye Tate Williams
Quan Williams
Dean Carlton Wilson
Greg Woods
Milton Wright

Index

THANK YOU

Antoine J. Alston, NCA&T, Associate Dean
Maseo Bolin, NCA&T, Player
Connie "Breeze" Boykin, NCCU, Player
Jessie Britt, NCA&T, Player
Chioke D. Brown, NCCU, Photographer
Coach Vincent Brown, NCA&T
Wheeler Brown, NCA&T, Player
Douglas Burt, Douglas Burt Photography
The Charlotte Sports Foundation
Dr. Kimberley Cheek, NCA&T, Graduate Research Assistant
Miranda Clinton, NCCU, Undergraduate Research Assistant
Patrick Cullom, UNC, Wilson Library
Charles L. Curry, Jr., Contributor
Rodney Dawson, Greensboro History Museum
Jacqueline Dean, UNC, Wilson Library
Curtis Deloatch, NCAT, Player
Department of Athletics, NCA&T
Department of Athletics, NCCU
Monique Douglas, Brooklyn Collective
Kevin L. Dorsey, Kevin L. Dorsey Photography
Beverly Barnes Evans, Contributor
Vann Evans, State Archives of North Carolina
Dr. Jerry Gershenhorn, NCCU, Professor
Valerie Gillispie, Duke University, University Archivist
Isaac Green, NCCU
Greensboro History Museum
Spencer Gwynn, NCA&T
Evonda Haith, NCA&T
Earl Hilton, III, NCA&T, Athletic Director
Irwin Holmes, Jr., Contributor
Meredythe Holmes, Contributor
Dennis Homesley, NCA&T, Player
Alan Hooker, NCA&T, Player
Dr. David H. Jackson, Jr., NCCU, Provost
Ryan Jackson, NCCU, Graduate Research Assistant
Carla D. Johnson, Contributor
Michael Johnson, NCCU
Edwin Jones, NCCU
Will Lawson, Charlotte Sports Foundation
Dr. Harold L. Martin, Sr., NCA&T Chancellor
Kyrie Mason, NCCU, Graduate Research Assistant
Naitara Matthews, NCCU, Undergraduate Research Assistant

Atty. H.M. "Mickey" Michaux, NCCU
June Michaux, NCCU
Atty. Eric Montgomery, NCCU
Museum of Durham History
NCA&T Alumni Association
NCCU Alumni Association
Coach Trei Oliver, NCCU
Dr. Louis "Skip" Perkins, NCCU, Athletic Director
Dr. James Pilgrim, NCCU
Jay Pilgrim, Contributor
Juanita Pilgrim, NCCU
William "Billy" Reid, NCCU, Player
Kaleah Rogers, Charlotte Sports Foundation
Clara Scarborough, NCCU
Serba Kyle, NCCU, Deputy Athletics Director for External Affairs
Jeanette Shaffer, Museum of Durham History
Dr. Michael Simmons, NCA&T
Dallas Simmons, Jr., NCCU
Maurice Smith, NCA&T, Player
Dr. Tonya Smith-Jackson, NCA&T, Provost
Rebecca Stubbs-Carter, UNC, Wilson Library
Lula Thorpe, NCCU
Jason Tomberlin, UNC, Wilson Library
Mitzi Townes, NCCU, Graduate Research Assistant
Andre Vann, NCCU, Coordinator of University Archives
Coach Sam Washington, NCA&T
Darien Wellman, NCA&T, Graduate Research Assistant
Dr. Ingrid Wicker-McCree, NCCU, Athletic Director
Atty. James "Butch" Williams, NCCU
Kamilah Henry Williams, NCA&T, Undergraduate Research Assistant
Orilonise Yarborough, NCCU, Graduate Research Assistant
Miller Yoho, Charlotte Sports Foundation
GeColby Youngblood, NCCU, Graduate Research Assistant